Chic & Unique
VINTAGE
Cakes

ZOE CLARK

D&C
David and Charles

www.stitchcraftcreate.co.uk/ideas/kitchen

Contents

Introduction

'Vintage' has become highly popular – especially when it comes to occasion and wedding cakes – so now seemed the perfect time to explore this theme. I had so much fun researching and creating the intricate and beautiful vintage cakes within this book.

So, what exactly does 'vintage' mean? Items such as clothing, furniture and household objects that range between 20–100 years old and are representative of the era in which they have been made can be given the label 'vintage'.

Most of the cakes in this book are set around vintage styles, from the flapper dresses of the Charleston era through to 1950s big skirts and tight bodices. With projects ranging from simplistic tiered cakes to more complex, novelty creations, I have aimed to cater for all tastes and have tailored my designs to intermediate level sugarcrafters and above.

Following the *Chic and Unique* series, this book features ten main projects, each illustrated with clear step-by-step instructions and photography to show you how to recreate the cakes. It is important to read the whole chapter before you start, as some elements may need to be prepared up to 24–48 hours in advance.

Each chapter contains two alternative projects to make when time is short, or if you would like a little something to accompany the main designs. You will also discover a wealth of useful tips, technique information and recipes. I hope my ideas will inspire you and you will enjoy creating your own truly timeless, vintage creations.

Zoe
x

TOOLS AND EQUIPMENT

The following checklists contain all of the essential basic tools for baking the cakes in this book, plus any tools that you will need for your creative work. Keep all your tools and equipment to hand before you start baking. Any specific tools that are required in addition to the basics are listed in the individual projects.

Baking essentials

- ❖ **Large electric mixer** for making cakes, buttercream (frosting) and royal icing
- ❖ **Kitchen scales** for weighing out ingredients
- ❖ **Measuring spoons** for measuring small quantities
- ❖ **Mixing bowls** for mixing ingredients
- ❖ **Spatulas** for mixing and gently folding together cake mixes
- ❖ **Cake tins** for baking cakes
- ❖ **Cupcake or muffin trays** for baking cupcakes
- ❖ **Baking trays** for baking cookies
- ❖ **Wire racks** for cooling cakes

GENERAL EQUIPMENT

- ❖ **Greaseproof (wax) paper or baking parchment** for lining tins and to use under icing during preparation
- ❖ **Clingfilm (plastic wrap)** for covering icing to prevent drying out and for wrapping cookie dough
- ❖ **Large non-stick board** to put icing on when rolling it out (alternatively you may roll out icing on a workbench using a dusting of icing sugar to prevent sticking)
- ❖ **Non-slip mat** to put under the board so that it doesn't slip on the work surface
- ❖ **Large and small non-stick rolling pins** for rolling out icing and marzipan
- ❖ **Large and small sharp knife or scalpel** for cutting and shaping icing
- ❖ **Large serrated knife** for carving and sculpting cakes
- ❖ **Cake leveller** for cutting even, level layers of sponge
- ❖ **Large and small palette knife** for applying buttercream (frosting) and ganache
- ❖ **Icing or marzipan spacers** to give a guide to the thickness of icing and marzipan when rolling out
- ❖ **Icing smoothers** for smoothing icing
- ❖ **Spirit level** for checking that cakes are level when stacking them
- ❖ **Metal ruler** for measuring different heights and lengths
- ❖ **Kitchen towel/tissue** for drying off brushes
- ❖ **Cake scraper** to scrape and smooth buttercream (frosting), ganache or royal icing, used in a similar way to a palette knife

Creative tools and materials

- **Hollow plastic dowels** for assembling cakes

- **Turntable** for layering cakes

- **Double-sided tape** to attach ribbon around cakes, boards and pillars

- **Piping (pastry) bags**, paper or plastic, for royal icing decorations and piping swirls on cupcakes

- **Piping tubes (tips)**, nos. 1 and 1.5, for royal icing decorations

- **Cocktail sticks (toothpicks) or cel sticks** for colouring and curling icing

- **Edible glue** for sticking icing to icing

- **Edible pens** for marking positioning guides

- **Needle scriber** for lightly scoring positioning guides and bursting bubbles in icing

- **Cake-top marking template** for finding/marking the centre of cakes and marking where dowels should be placed

- **Pastry brush** for brushing sugar syrup and apricot masking spread or strained jam (jelly) on to cakes

- **Fine paintbrushes** for gluing and painting

- **Dusting brushes** for brushing edible dust on to icing

- **Ball tool** for frilling or thinning the edge of flower (petal/gum) paste

- **Foam pad** for softening and frilling flower (petal/gum) paste

- **Circle cutters** for cutting circles of various sizes

- **Shaped cutters** for cutting out shapes such as flowers, ovals and hearts for icing and cookies

- **Clear alcohol** for mixing into dust to paint on icing and for sticking icing to marzipan

- **Trex (white vegetable fat)** for greasing the board, pins and moulds

DUSKY LACE DREAM

Lace wedding dresses have always been classically popular and since Kate Middleton wore a lacy gown on her wedding day, they now seem to be even more on trend. So many of my brides want a wedding cake that matches the theme of their dress and it's one of my favourite ways to decorate a cake; making a beautiful creation that's also tailored to them.

Although I wouldn't call the style of lace in these designs particularly vintage; the colour scheme, with its romantic dusky pink hues and delicate ivory detailing is certainly classic. With its exquisite floral lace design, soft ribbon trim and the subtle hint of sparkle from the pearl white lustre, this really is the wedding cake of dreams.

Beautiful bridal lace

It is all about the detail with this sophisticated three-tiered wedding cake design. The elegant floral lace pattern is created using a combination of appliqué techniques, including a type of piping that resembles embroidery in its method of creating tiny zigzags and lines. The use of a lace mould adds texture to give a realistic finish. Tiny teardrops are added for the beading on the large flowers and edible pearls bring that extra wow-factor to the cake.

MATERIALS

* One 13cm (5in) round cake (see *Cake Recipes*), 10cm (4in) deep and one 23cm (9in) round cake, 11.5cm (4⅜in) deep, prepared and iced in ivory sugarpaste (rolled fondant) (see *Covering with Marzipan and Sugarpaste*)

* One 18cm (7in) round cake, 13cm (5in) deep, iced in pale dusky pink sugarpaste (rolled fondant) (see *Covering with Marzipan and Sugarpaste*)

* One 30cm (12in) round cake board, covered with ivory sugarpaste (rolled fondant) (see *Icing Cake Boards*)

* 1kg (2lb 4oz) pale dusky pink sugarpaste (rolled fondant) (the same colour as the paste used to ice the middle tier)

* Half quantity of royal icing (see *Royal Icing*)

* 15ml (1 tbsp) each of royal icing in dusky pink and ivory to match cakes

* Edible white pearl dragées

* 100g (3½oz) white flower (petal/gum) paste

* Pearl white lustre

* White non toxic/edible glitter

EQUIPMENT

* Card

* 7 hollow pieces of dowel cut to size (see *Assembling Tiered Cakes*)

* Large flower template (see *Templates*)

* Pins

* Piping bag (see *Making a Piping Bag*) and nos. 1, 1.5 and 4 piping tubes (tips)

* Scallop edge cutter (Orchard Products)

* Lace mould or textured mat (CK)

* 3 small size primrose cutters

* 2 small blossom plunger cutters

* 1.5cm (⅝in) ivory/bridal white, double-faced satin ribbon

1 Roll out about 200g (7oz) of dusky pink sugarpaste (rolled fondant) into a long strip measuring 50 x 7.5 x 0.2cm (20 x 3 x 1/16in). Cut down one side of the strip with a knife to achieve a straight edge, then wrap and glue the paste around the 13cm (5in) tier. Cut a piece of card to 6cm (2½in) in height and use to neatly score and cut away the icing above this height all around the cake to form an even band. Set aside to dry for a few hours or ideally overnight – this should be done on the same day as you ice the cakes.

TIP

To hide the join in the sugarpaste (rolled fondant) strip, trim it at the back and blend the icing together using your fingers.

2 Roll out the remaining dusky pink sugarpaste (rolled fondant) to a 2mm (1/16in) thickness and cover the top of the 23cm (9in) tier. Use your hands to smooth the icing down around the sides until about halfway down. Cut another piece of card about 7.5cm (3in) in height and use to make a level cut in the icing all the way around the cake, this time working from the top down. Continue smoothing the icing against the cake, trimming the bottom if it becomes slightly out of shape. Set aside to dry for a few hours or overnight.

3 Dowel and assemble the three tiers on the iced cake board (see *Assembling Tiered Cakes*).

4 Using an edible pen, trace the large flower template (see *Templates*) onto greaseproof (wax) paper ten or eleven times. Pin each one onto the cake, spacing them evenly apart and positioning each flower at a different angle. Secure each template in place using four pins. Using a needle scriber, prick through each flower to mark its outline on the cake. Carefully remove the paper and pins, putting them safely away.

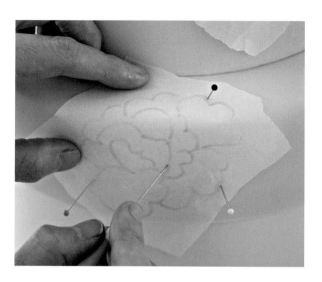

5 Use a no. 1 piping tube (tip) and fill a piping bag with soft peak royal icing then pipe over the design (see *Piping with Royal Icing*). Your piping should not be perfect; aim for a bumpy stop-and-start effect, such as in embroidery or stitching. Next, pipe tiny adjoining pairs of teardrops around the outside of each flower.

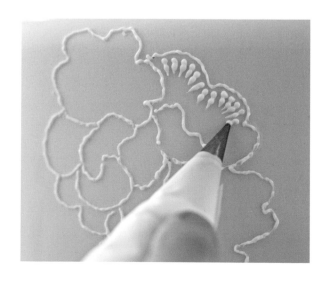

6 Use a ball tool to make some small round indents in the centre of the flowers then press in some pearl dragées, using a little edible glue to secure in place.

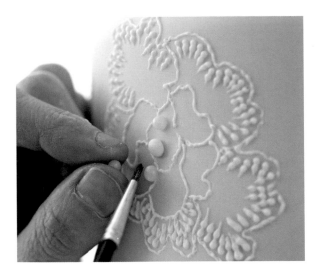

7 For the scallop edging around the top and bottom tiers, roll out some white flower (petal/gum) paste into a long, 7mm (⅜in) thick strip and use the scallop cutter to cut out a border. Add texture by pressing the scalloped pieces into a lace mould, brushed first with pearl white lustre to prevent the paste from sticking and to give it shine. Alternatively, press the pieces into a textured mat and paint them with pearl white lustre mixed with clear alcohol. Use edible glue to attach the trim around the top tier with the curved edge upwards and around the bottom tier with the curved edge downwards.

TIP

Try to make the scallop-edged pieces fairly long, but don't worry too much if they are shorter as you can easily join the pieces together.

8 For the smaller appliqué flowers, thinly roll out some white flower (petal/gum) paste and press it into the lace mould, as in Step 7. Cut out a flower with the largest primrose cutter and use the smallest primrose cutter to cut out the centre. Use the largest blossom plunger cutter to cut out the centre of the medium primrose and the smaller blossom plunger cutter to cut out the centre of the smallest primrose. You can save the cut out centres and use them to decorate the cake.

9 Attach the appliqué flowers on to the cake with edible glue, using the main photograph as a guide for positioning. Attach the largest blossoms into the centre of the largest primroses and use a ball tool to indent the centres before the flower (petal/gum) paste dries. Glue white pearl dragées into the indents.

10 Roll out some more white flower (petal/gum) paste and leave it to dry for about five minutes. Use a no. 4 piping tube (tip) to cut out lots of tiny little dots – these will resemble sequins on the cake. Stick them on to the cake in the centre of the little flowers and around the outside of the larger flowers using edible glue.

11 Mix some pearl white lustre with alcohol and paint all the sequins and the teardrop piping on the main flowers. Brush a small amount of edible glue on to the central dragée on the larger flowers and dab on some glitter with a paintbrush to make it sparkle.

12 Fill a piping bag with a no. 1.5 tube (tip) and pipe the snail trail borders (see *Piping with Royal Icing*) around each tier, using dusky pink royal icing for the top two tiers and ivory royal icing for the bottom tier.

13 Carefully pipe the leaves using a piping bag with a no. 1 tube (tip) and white royal icing. Pipe the main leaf shape first, then zigzag back and forth to fill the leaf in.

TIP

Pipe your zigzags in a similar way to sewing stitches; making some lines very pointed and other lines more curved.

14 Finish by wrapping and securing some white, double-faced satin ribbon around the cake board (see *Securing Ribbon Around Cakes and Boards*).

Pretty appliqué cupcakes

These sweet and stylish lace cupcakes perfectly complement the main design, simply using the small appliqué flowers to embellish the dusky pink sugarpaste covering. They almost look too pretty to eat!

Simply decorate the cupcakes using the appliqué flowers, made in the same way as for the *Beautiful Bridal Lace* cake, following Steps 8–10. Carefully pipe the leaves around the flowers using a piping bag with a no. 1 tube (tip) and white royal icing. Pipe the main leaf shape first, then zigzag back and forth to fill the leaf in. Paint the sequins with pearl lustre mixed with alcohol.

YOU'LL ALSO NEED

❖ Cupcakes (see *Baking Cupcakes*) in silver foil cases, iced with a disc of dusky pink sugarpaste (rolled fondant) (see *Covering Cupcakes with Sugarpaste*)

❖ Appliqué flowers (see Steps 8–10, *Beautiful Bridal Lace*)

❖ White royal icing (see *Royal Icing*)

❖ Piping bag (see *Making a Piping Bag*) and no. 1 tube (tip)

❖ Pearl lustre mixed with clear alcohol

Floral lace cookies

These cute heart-shaped cookies would make wonderful wedding favours or Valentine's Day gifts. The larger flower from the main cake design is used, with its pretty teardrop details and intricately piped petals and leaves giving a truly romantic feel.

Scribe the design onto the cookie (see Step 4, *Beautiful Bridal Lace*). Fill a piping bag with a no.1 piping tube (tip) with soft peak royal icing and pipe over the design in the same way as for the main cake. Pipe the leaf shapes, zigzagging back and forth to fill them in.

Press in some pearl dragées (see Step 6, *Beautiful Bridal Lace*) then add the sequins (see Step 10, *Beautiful Bridal Lace*), securing them on to the cookies as shown. Mix some pearl white lustre with alcohol and paint all the sequins and the teardrop piping. Finally, brush a small amount of glue onto the central dragée and dab on some glitter with a paintbrush.

YOU'LL ALSO NEED

- 10cm (4in) wide heart cookies (see *Baking Cookies*) iced with dusky pink sugarpaste (rolled fondant) (see *Covering Cookies with Sugarpaste*), ideally 24 hours in advance

- Piping bag (see *Making a Piping Bag*) and nos. 1 and 4 piping tubes (tips)

- Large flower template (see *Templates*)

- White royal icing (see *Royal Icing*)

- Pearl lustre

- White edible pearl dragées

- Non toxic/edible glitter

VINTAGE JEWELS

Vintage jewellery is so popular today, from gorgeous cameo brooches and elaborate hairpins to timeless pearls and sparkling gemstone rings. Looking at the tempting array of classic adornments around, I was eager to replicate their beauty through sugarcraft. The huge variety of vintage jewellery moulds now available will leave you spoilt for choice.

I didn't just want to stop at the jewellery – what better way to display this collection of goodies than with a gorgeous jewellery box case? With its classic caramel-coffee colour, stylish embossed rose details, pretty trims and classic lace-covered board, this will be the perfect home for all your vintage jewellery creations.

Classic jewellery box

This stunning jewellery box cake design features an open drawer for you to place your vintage jewellery inside, made by cutting out a chunk from the cake. It is designed with an opening lid, created using a foam board with a layer of cake on top and placing a dowel inside the cake to form a gap, however you can omit this stage to create a more simplistic closed box design.

MATERIALS

- One 33cm (13in) round cake board, covered with medium-dark brown sugarpaste (rolled fondant) (see *Icing Cake Boards*)

- Paste food colouring: medium-brown, black

- 35cm (14in) square cake baked with 650g (1lb 7oz) sponge mix (see *Cake Recipes*), trimmed to 4cm (1½in) deep and cut up into three rectangles, each measuring 19 x 12.5cm (7½ x 5in)

- 19 x 12.5 x 4cm (7½ x 5 x 1½in) cake dummy (optional)

- One quantity of ganache (see *Ganache*)

- 1kg (2lb 4oz) caramel-coffee coloured sugarpaste (rolled fondant)

- Half quantity of royal icing (see *Royal Icing*)

- Flower (petal/gum) paste: 30g (1⅛oz) pale ivory, 30g (1⅛oz) white, 30g (1⅛oz) caramel-coloured, 20g (¾oz) coral-coloured (made by mixing pink and peach), 30g (1⅛oz) grey

- Lustres: pearl white, ivory pearl, silver, gold

- Piece of Rose Mantilla Sugarveil (see *Using Sugarveil*)

EQUIPMENT

- Two pieces of 5mm (¼in) width foam board, 19 x 12.5cm (7½ x 5in)

- Tea Rose patchwork cutter

- One piece of 5mm (¼in) foam board, 12 x 4.5cm (4¾ x 1¾in)

- One thin dowel cut to size (see *Assembling Tiered Cakes*)

- Moulds: Perfect Pearl (First Impressions), Filigree Butterflies (FPC), Filigree Brooches (FPC), Three Brooches (FPC), Cameo Ladies (FPC)

- Large lace mould (CK)

- Lace cutter set (Orchard Products)

- 4cm (1½in) oval cutter

- 1.5cm (⅝in) pale coffee, double-faced satin ribbon

1 Use a flat paintbrush to paint the cake board with medium-brown paste food colouring diluted with water. Set aside to dry.

2 Attach one layer of cake onto a 19 x 12.5cm (7½ x 5in) piece of foam board using a small amount of ganache. Cut out a piece from a second cake layer on one side, 2.5cm (1in) in from each end and 2cm (¾in) deep.

3 Use ganache to attach the cut layer on top of a third cake layer. Thinly spread ganache where the drawer section is cut and continue across the front of the box.

4 Roll out 150g (5½oz) of caramel-coffee sugarpaste (rolled fondant). Cover the section where the drawer will be placed and carefully trim. Turn the cake upside down and attach it to the other 19 x 12.5cm (7½ x 5in) foam board with ganache. Thinly cover the cake and lid with ganache and place them briefly in the fridge to firm up.

5 Roll out 700g (1lb 9oz) of caramel-coffee sugarpaste (rolled fondant) to 4mm (½in) thick and cover the box (see *Covering with Marzipan and Sugarpaste*). Cut out the drawer section with a small sharp knife or scalpel then cover the lid as before, trimming any excess. Roll out leftover paste to 3mm (⅛in) thick and cover the exposed foam board, measuring the area first and trimming any excess. Press the Tea Rose patchwork cutter into the icing to mark it while it is still soft. Mark one on the front, one on each side, two on the lid and one on the back.

6 Check that the 12 x 4.5cm (4¾ x 1¾in) foam board fits inside the drawer, allowing for a 4mm (⅛in) gap on each side. Trim if necessary with a scalpel. Roll out 75g (2¾oz) of caramel-coffee coloured sugarpaste (rolled fondant) to 3mm (⅛in), cover the small foam board (see *Icing Cake Boards*) and set aside.

7 Mix 2.5ml (½tsp) CMC (Tylose) into 150g (5½oz) of caramel-coffee coloured sugarpaste (rolled fondant) so it becomes quite hard (see *Modelling Paste and CMC*). Roll out the paste to 3mm (⅛in) thick and cut out the drawer sides: cut out the two sides first, using the base of the drawer as a guide and measuring the height by checking the gap in the cake. Next, cut out the front and back – both pieces will need to be slightly longer than the actual length of the drawer as they will also need to cover the sides. Set aside to dry before attaching them on to the base with edible glue. Attach the two sides in place first, then the front and back.

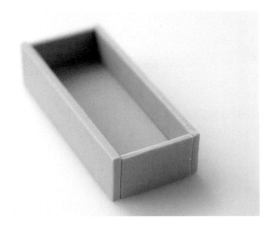

8 Cover most of board with a piece of 'Rose Mantilla' Sugarveil (see *Using Sugarveil*), trimming it to fit with a scalpel and moistening a little with water if necessary.

9 Position the cake slightly off-centre on the board, securing it with royal icing. Place a thin dowel into the centre. Mark it about 5mm (¼in) higher than the top of the cake then remove it, cut it and put it back in. Attach the lid with royal icing – it should rest on the back ledge of the cake and the dowel. Trim the dowel if it is visible.

10 To make the trim for the bottom of the lid, thinly roll out the ivory flower (petal/gum) paste to 1mm (¹⁄₁₆in) thick and 20cm (8in) long and use the lace mould to indent texture into the paste (see Step 7, *Beautiful Bridal Lace*). Use the lace trim cutter to cut out a pointed edge and use a sharp knife to cut a straight edge down the other side. Attach with the pointed edge facing upwards around the base of the lid using edible glue, then continue to attach the trim around the lid, making the joins as neat as possible. Repeat around the top of the cake, just below the gap, with the pointed edge facing down. Roll out some more paste, indent with the lace and use the cutter to cut a length of paste with both sides pointed. Measure the length of the drawer face and cut the icing to fit. Attach it in place with edible glue then secure the drawer into place with royal icing.

11 Roll a tiny ball from caramel flower (petal/gum) paste and attach onto the centre of the drawer. Press another tiny amount into the central part of the one of the brooches from the Three Brooches mould, pop it out and stick it onto the ball for the handle. Thinly roll out the rest of the paste and cut out two rectangles for the hinges, each measuring 2 x 1.5cm (¾ x ⅝in). Secure in place with edible glue then use a no. 4 piping tube (tip) to indent the screws at each corner. Roll tiny sausages, trim them to go across the centre of each hinge and indent vertical lines across them with a small sharp knife.

Butterfly hair pin

Colour 20g (¾oz) of white flower (petal/gum) paste with black paste food colouring to make a grey shade. Roll out a long thick piece and cut it to about 3mm (⅛in) wide with a sharp knife. Make a small indent all the way down both sides of the clip to resemble two pieces and cut a point in one end. Press tiny pieces of white flower (petal/gum) paste into the pearl details of the Filigree Butterflies mould then use grey flower (petal/gum) paste to fill the rest of the mould (see *Using Moulds*). Pop the icing out then cut out around the antennae. Attach the moulded icing onto the pin with edible glue. Once dry, paint over the grey flower (petal/gum) paste with silver lustre and the pearls with white lustre.

Cameo necklace

For the cameo, press a little white flower (petal/gum) paste into the head detail of the 3.5cm (1⅜in) Cameo Ladies mould. Press some grey flower (petal/gum) paste on top to fill the remainder then pop out the cameo. Roll out some caramel-coffee coloured flower (petal/gum) paste to 3mm (⅛in) thick and cut out the back using an oval cutter. Secure the cameo on top with edible glue.

For the chain, roll out a thin, 1.5cm (⅝in) long sausage shape for the hook, trim and secure in place with edible glue. Paint the hook and the back of the cameo with gold lustre. To make the chain, roll a thin sausage to 40cm (16in) long. Make indentations all the way along one side with the end of a paintbrush then repeat on the other side. Make a quarter turn and repeat for this side then turn and repeat again if necessary. While the icing is still soft, secure the chain through the hook of the cameo and secure it in place on the cake with edible glue, going from inside the drawer out onto the board.

Pearls

The coral and white strings of pearls are made with white and coral-coloured flower (petal/gum) paste in the same way as described in Step 3, *Fabulous Feathers Cake*. Brush white lustre into the mould first for both colours. Stick the coral pearls into the drawer and attach the white pearls to appear trapped between the lid and the box, draping out onto the board.

Earrings

Simply press grey flower (petal/gum) paste into the middle brooch of the Filigree Brooches mould, then paint the central part with black paste food colouring and the outer part with silver lustre. Stick them into the box with edible glue or royal icing if they are too dry.

Brooch clasp

Press white flower (petal/gum) paste into the central oval pearl part of the mould, then fill the rest with caramel (petal/gum) paste. Pop it out then attach it onto the cake with edible glue. Paint the central part with white lustre and the outside with gold lustre.

12 Paint the necklace chain and hinges with gold lustre then mix the pale ivory lustre with alcohol and paint over the roses. Finish by placing the butterfly clip in the drawer or on the board (secured in place with edible glue if you like) and attach some ribbon around the board (see *Securing Ribbon Around Cakes and Boards*).

YOU'LL ALSO NEED

❖ 6 x 5cm (2½ x 2in) deep square miniature un-iced cakes (see *Miniature Square Cakes*)

❖ Sugarpaste (rolled fondant): ivory, brown

❖ Flower (petal/gum) paste: pale coffee, grey

❖ Black food paste colouring

Precious ring mini cake

This stunning ring box mini cake is the perfect accompaniment to the main jewellery box cake or can be given to celebrate an engagement. Although there is a generous amount of icing in comparison to cake, it will undoubtedly make a gorgeous gift for that special occasion.

Cover the top of the cake with a small square of ivory sugarpaste (rolled fondant) about 3–4mm (⅛in) thick. Make a slit in the sugarpaste (rolled fondant) with a sharp knife and tease it open slightly for the ring to sit in. Add a small amount of CMC (Tylose) to the brown sugarpaste (rolled fondant) to stiffen it, then roll out the paste to 2mm (¹⁄₁₆in) thick and cut out the sides of the box. Cut the opposite sides first, then the other two. These should stick to the coating on the cake, although you can use edible glue if necessary where they join at the corners. Make the lid in the same way: cut out the top square first then the sides and set aside to dry.

   Make the pointed trim around the box and lid (see Step 10, *Classic Jewellery Box*) using the pale coffee coloured flower (petal/gum) paste. Roll a tiny sausage from grey flower (petal/gum) paste and cut it to about 3cm (1¼in). Let it harden a little in a curved position to holds its shape then measure it, trim if necessary, and position in the slit in the ivory icing. Make the top of the ring in the same way as for the earrings (see *Classic Jewellery Box, Earrings*)

Cameo and brooch cookies

These simple, royal iced, oval-shaped cookies are glammed up with elements from the jewels found within the Classic Jewellery Box. The end result is irresistible!

Brush wet gold lustre over the caramel-iced cookie using even strokes and a flat brush. Secure the cameo into the centre of the cookie using a small amount of royal icing or edible glue if the cameo is still soft. Pipe dots of soft peak caramel-coloured royal icing around the cameo. When the dots are dry, paint over them with gold lustre using a fine paintbrush.

For the brooch cookie, simply stick the brooch to the pale coffee-coloured icing with some royal icing or edible glue if the brooch is still soft.

YOU'LL ALSO NEED

* 6cm (2¼in) oval-shaped cookies (see *Baking Cookies*), iced in caramel and pale coffee-coloured royal icing (see *Royal-Iced Cookies*)

* Piping bag (see *Making a Piping Bag*) with no. 1.5 tube (tip) filled with soft peak caramel-coloured royal icing (see *Piping with Royal Icing*)

* Gold lustre mixed with clear alcohol

* Cameo (see *Classic Jewellery Box, Cameo Necklace*)

* Brooch (see *Classic Jewellery Box, Brooch Clasp*)

* Royal icing or edible glue

DESIGNER ART DECO

Art Deco is a bold, eclectic style that originated in the 1920s and flourished during the 1930s–40s, combining traditional craft motifs with Machine Age imagery. As a movement, it represented luxury and glamour and embraced technological progress with its simple, classic shapes, repeating patterns, rich colour schemes and focus on symmetry.

I love Art Deco as a style and was eager to incorporate this classic theme into my own designs. I chose to use a striking black, gold and ivory colour scheme, which oozes style and sophistication. The repetitive patterns can be made more quickly and easily than you would imagine with the help of Art Deco templates and stencils.

Symmetrical shapes cake

I designed this tall, tiered cake with Art Deco architecture in mind. Its shape is very angular, reminiscent of Art Deco buildings, and by adding gaps between the tiers a long, elegant structure is produced. To make the bold Art Deco motifs and patterns, I used a stencil to create a repetitive, symmetrical design; an effective technique that is so much quicker than cutting out individual pieces. For best results, transport the cake in separate tiers and assemble it in situ.

MATERIALS

❖ One 10cm (4in) square cake (see *Cake Recipes*), 9.5cm (3¾in) deep; one 12.5cm (5in) square cake, 10cm (4in) deep; one 23cm (6in) square cake, 11cm (4¼in) deep; and one 20cm (8in) square cake, 12cm (4¾in) deep, each prepared and iced in ivory sugarpaste (rolled fondant) at least 12–24 hours in advance (see *Covering with Marzipan and Sugarpaste*)

❖ One 25cm (10in) square cake board, covered with black sugarpaste (rolled fondant) (see *Icing Cake Boards*)

❖ Flower (petal/gum) paste: 800g (1lb 12oz) caramel-coloured, 600g (1lb 5oz) black

❖ Gold lustre

❖ One quantity of royal icing (see *Royal Icing*)

❖ Paste food colouring: black and caramel/ivory

EQUIPMENT

❖ 12 hollow pieces of dowel cut to size (see *Assembling Tiered Cakes*)

❖ 7.5cm (3in) by 2.5cm (1in) deep square polystyrene cake dummy

❖ Two 10cm (4in), two 12.5cm (5in) and two 18cm (7in) square boards (drums), each pair stuck together with royal icing

❖ Art Deco stencil (Designer Stencils)

❖ Masking tape

❖ Templates A–F (see *Templates*)

❖ Oval cutter set (Ateco)

❖ Small oval cutters: 1.5cm (⅝in) and 2.5cm (1in) (measured lengthways)

❖ Square cutters: 2cm (¾in) and 8mm (⅜in)

❖ 2.5cm (1in) gold satin ribbon

❖ 1.5cm (⅝in) black, double-faced satin ribbon

1 Dowel the bottom three tiers of the cake (see *Assembling Tiered Cakes*), using four dowels in each tier. Notice that the board sitting on top of the dowelled tiers is smaller than the cake to be placed on top, so take care not to place the dowels too far apart.

2 To decorate the bottom tier, roll out about 50g (1¾oz) of caramel-coloured flower (petal/gum) paste to 1mm (¹⁄₁₆in) thick, flip it over and immediately dust it with gold lustre. Take your stencil and use masking tape to create a symmetrical rectangular frame, measuring 9 x 20cm (3½ x 8in).

3 Colour approximately 75ml (5 tbsp) of royal icing with black paste food colouring, then place the stencil over the dusted caramel flower (petal/gum) paste. Smear the icing over the paste using a palette knife and remove any excess icing.

4 Carefully peel the stencil away then cut out the rectangle with a sharp knife, leaving a 1–2mm (¹⁄₁₆in) gap all the way around the stencilled pattern. Set aside until the royal icing is dry but there is still a bend in the paste. Repeat to make three more stencilled rectangles; one for each side. Use edible glue to secure the four rectangular pieces onto each side, 12mm (½in) from the bottom of the cake. Cover the icing with a damp cloth whilst you are working to prevent a crust from forming.

TIP

You may need to wash the stencil each time it is used, however the masking tape should stay in place.

5 Thinly roll out 75g (2¾oz) of black flower (petal/gum) paste and cut out four ovals with the 8.5cm (3⅜in) cutter, four with the 6cm (2¼in) cutter and four with the 4cm (1¾in) cutter. You will probably need to re-roll the paste and perhaps add to it, to cut all of them out. Repeat with the caramel flower (petal/gum) paste using the 8cm (3¼in), 5.5cm (2¼in) and 3cm (1¼in) cutters, flipping and brushing the paste with gold lustre before cutting out. Stick the smallest gold oval onto the smallest black oval, the second smallest gold oval onto the second smallest black oval, and so on. Using edible glue, attach the ovals together in a line with the smallest at the top, overlapping them as you go down to the largest one. When all the pieces are joined together, cut the bottom oval flat horizontally and attach it on to the corner of the cake so the flat edge sits flush with the bottom. Repeat for each corner.

6 To make the decorative trim around the base of the cake, roll out some black flower (petal/gum) paste and cut out small ovals using the 1.5cm (⅝in) and 2.5cm (1in) cutters. You will need about ten large and eight small ovals. Cut them in half widthways with a small sharp knife then stick them around the base of the cake with edible glue.

7 The second tier down is made in the same way as the bottom tier but on a slightly smaller scale. The rectangular shape is 7.5 x 13cm (3 x 5in), so you will need to adjust your masking tape frame to fit this size. The oval shapes on the corners of the cake are cut using one size smaller cutters for each piece (8cm (3¼in), 5.5cm (2¼in), and 3cm (1¼in) cutters for the black ovals and 7cm (2¾in), 5cm (2in) and 2.5cm (1in) cutters for the gold ovals). You will also need fewer small ovals for the edging around the base of the tier.

8 To decorate the top tier, start by thinly rolling out about 60g (2¼oz) of black flower (petal/gum) paste. Use Template C (see *Templates*) to cut out four wide diamond shapes from one side of the paste and set aside. Roll out about 40g (1½oz) of caramel flower (petal/gum) paste to the same thickness, flip it over and dust it with gold lustre. Cut out four more diamond shapes using Template B (see *Templates*) and set aside.

TIP

Use a cake dummy for the top or even the top two tiers if you'd like it to be a little less precarious!

9 Take Template A (see *Templates*) and place it under the Art Deco stencil. Use masking tape to frame the kite shape: it should be about 1–2mm (⅟₁₆in) in from the edge of the template. Take the stencil off the template. Colour 30ml (2 tbsp) of royal icing with caramel paste food colour. Roll out some additional black flower (petal/gum) paste and place the stencil on top. Smear a thin layer of the caramel icing over the diamond shape using a palette knife and carefully scrape away the excess. Lift off the stencil to reveal the diamond shape with stencilled pattern then cut around it using a sharp knife, leaving a 1–2mm (⅟₁₆in) gap around the pattern. Repeat four times and set aside to dry a little.

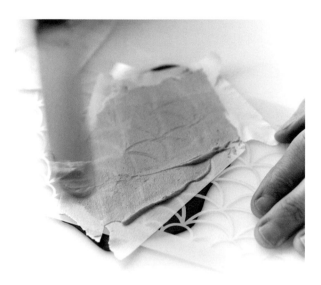

10 Stick all three cut out kite shapes together with the stencilled one on top, the caramel gold dusted one in the middle and the black one underneath. Attach them onto the centre of each side of the cake, about 5–7mm (¼in) up from the bottom.

11 To make the decorative trim around the base, thinly roll out some more black flower (petal/gum) paste and cut out eight squares using the 2cm (¾in) cutter. Cut each square in half to make a triangle then secure them around the base of the cake with edible glue, placing them symmetrically on each side of the central main design. Roll out some caramel flower (petal/gum) paste, turn it over, brush it with gold lustre and cut out eight

small squares using the 8mm (⅜in) square cutter. Secure them onto the cake in-between the small black triangles using edible glue.

12 The third tier down has the same design as the top tier. Repeat Steps 8–11 above, using templates D, E and F (see *Templates*) to make a larger central motif design. Mix some gold lustre with alcohol and paint the stencilled caramel royal icing on the top and third tier.

13 To assemble the cake, start by wrapping and securing some 2.5cm (1in) gold satin ribbon twice around the double cake boards and the 7.5cm (3in) cake dummy using double-sided tape (see *Securing Ribbon Around Cakes and Boards*).

14 Attach the two 17.5cm (7in) boards onto the centre of the iced black base board using royal icing. Let them set before carefully sticking on the bottom tier. Next attach on the 12.5cm (5in) boards, followed by the 15cm (6in) tier, then attach the 10cm (4in) boards followed by the 12.5cm (5in) tier and finally the 7.5cm (3in) dummy and the top tier. Wait for each board and tier to set before securing on the next. Make sure the ends of the ribbon are hidden at the back of the cake.

15 Finish by wrapping and securing some black ribbon around the base board (see *Securing Ribbon Around Cakes and Boards*).

Geometric mini cakes

These bold mini cakes use simplified elements from the Symmetrical Shapes Cake to really make a statement. The detailed stencilling on the central motif has been omitted and a zigzag strip cutter is used to decorate the base, as a quick alternative to cutting out individual triangles.

Roll out a strip of black flower (petal/gum) paste to at least 23cm (9in) long and use a zigzag strip cutter to make a jagged edge along one side. Use a sharp knife to cut a straight edge along the other side then use edible glue to secure it with its straight side down around the base of the cake, trimming away any excess paste. Roll out some more black flower (petal/gum) paste and cut out four shapes using Templates G and four shapes using Template I (see *Templates*).

Roll out some caramel flower (petal/gum) paste, turn it over, brush it with gold lustre and cut out four kite shapes from template H (see *Templates*). Stick them together then attach to each side of the cake with edible glue, using the photograph as a guide.

YOU'LL ALSO NEED

✤ 5cm (2in) square miniature cakes iced in ivory sugarpaste (rolled fondant) (see *Miniature Square Cakes*)

✤ Flower (petal/gum) paste: black, caramel

✤ Zigzag strip cutter

✤ Templates G, H, I (see *Templates*)

✤ Gold lustre

Deco coaster cookies

These striking, patterned cookies will make trendy adornments for your coffee table. They are so quick to make, simply using an Art Deco stencil on a square iced cookie for truly eye-catching results.

Frame a 6cm (2½in) square area on the stencil using masking tape (see Step 2, *Symmetrical Shapes Cake*). Roll out some caramel flower (petal/gum) paste, flip it over and dust it with gold lustre. Place the stencil onto the paste and thinly smear some black royal icing over the pattern. Remove any excess paste and carefully peel away the stencil. Cut out the stencilled square with a sharp knife, or the correct-sized square cutter, leaving a small 1mm (1⁄16in) border from the edge of the pattern. Allow to dry a little before attaching it onto the cookie.

Repeat, reversing the colours for the black cookie. You will need to paint the caramel royal icing with gold lustre mixed with alcohol when it is dry.

YOU'LL ALSO NEED

❖ 7cm (2¾in) square cookies (see *Baking Cookies*), either covered in sugarpaste (rolled fondant) (see *Covering Cookies with Sugarpaste*) or outlined and flooded in ivory (see *Royal-Iced Cookies*)

❖ Masking tape

❖ Flower (petal/gum) paste: black, caramel

❖ Gold lustre mixed with clear alcohol

❖ Royal icing: black, caramel

❖ Art Deco stencil (Designer Stencils)

❖ Square cutter (optional)

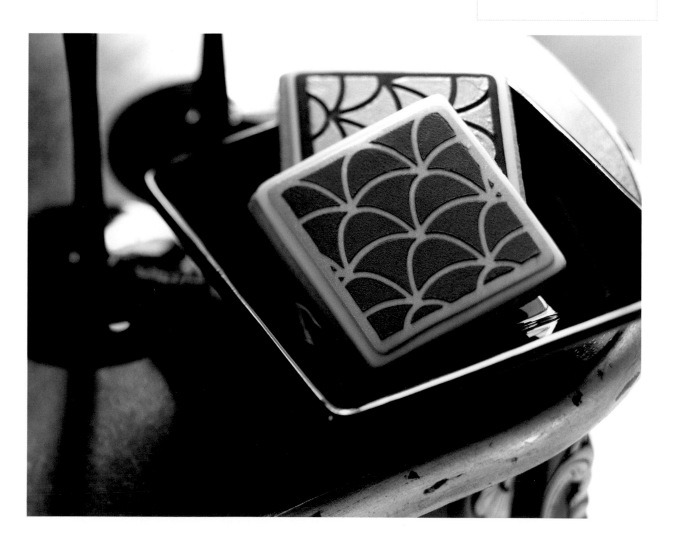

BEAUTIFUL HATBOXES

There is something intrinsically vintage about hatboxes. They take us back to the 1930s and 1940s, when ladies would proudly don wide-brimmed straw hats, decorative boaters and colourful berets. Vintage hatboxes have now become iconic collector's items, regarded as much for their beauty as the hats inside.

This painted floral design was inspired by a mix of vintage prints and fabrics used by modern-day designers. The rose pattern was inspired by a characteristic fabric from my favourite modern designer – as all my friends would tell you – Cath Kidston. This is essentially a 'vintage-style print', however I feel that the more vibrant use of colour and tone in the print gives it a slightly modern edge that really appeals.

Romantic rose hatbox

This floral hatbox cake has been iced using a slightly different method to achieve a surprisingly lifelike effect. When cutting away the sugarpaste (rolled fondant) on the side and top edges, the secret is to carefully angle your sharp knife to achieve a crisp and clean rim, then use a smoother to create a perfectly even finish to your sugarpaste covering. Although the idea of painting the roses can seem daunting, I have simplified the technique by focusing on the variations in colour depth where the petals and leaves face towards the light. I'm no painter, but this technique helps me to achieve pleasing results.

MATERIALS

❖ One 18cm (7in) round cake (see *Cake Recipes*), 12.5cm (5in) deep, layered, filled and coated with ganache or buttercream and chilled (see *Layering, Filling and Preparation*)

❖ One 33cm (13in) round cake board, covered with very pale grey sugarpaste (rolled fondant) (see *Icing Cake Boards*)

❖ 750g (1lb 10oz) pale blue sugarpaste (rolled fondant)

❖ Flower (petal/gum) paste: 125g (4½oz) pink, 50g (1¾oz) dusky pink, 20g (¾oz) caramel-coloured

❖ Edible pens: pink, green

❖ Dust: Superwhite or white

❖ Paste food colourings: ruby, foliage green

❖ 30ml (2 tbsp) royal icing (see *Royal Icing*)

❖ 50g (1¾oz) caramel-coloured sugarpaste (rolled fondant) mixed with 5ml (1 tsp) Trex (white vegetable fat) and 2.5ml (½ tsp) CMC (Tylose)

❖ Gold lustre mixed with clear alcohol

EQUIPMENT

❖ Large and small rose templates (see *Templates*)

❖ Plate

❖ Fine paintbrushes: nos. 0 and 2

❖ Sugar gun fitted with the largest rope attachment

❖ 5cm (2in), 6.5cm (2⅝oz) and 7.5cm (3in) petal rose cutters (FMM)

❖ Half bunch of gold stamen

❖ Paint palette former or apple tray

❖ Veining stick: Bark effect frilling tool (Jem)

❖ 1.5cm (⅝in) pink, double-faced satin ribbon

1 Place the cake onto some greaseproof (wax) paper, roll out about 700g (1lb 9oz) of pale blue sugarpaste (rolled fondant) and cover the cake (see *Covering with Marzipan and Sugarpaste*). Before you finish smoothing, use a sharp knife, angled on the horizontal, to go around the top edge of the cake and take off the icing.

2 Roll out the remaining sugarpaste (rolled fondant) together with any clean off-cuts from before and place it over the top of the cake. Smooth the top slightly then cut around the edge with the knife angled straight down to create a sharp edge around the cake. Level with icing smoothers and leave to dry, ideally for 24 hours.

3 Roll out the pink flower (petal/gum) paste into a long thin strip, 2mm (¹⁄₁₆in) thick and at least 65cm (26in) long. Using a large ruler or baton to help you, cut both sides of the strip with a sharp knife so it is 3cm (1¼in) wide. Brush a small amount of edible glue around the top of the cake and carefully stick the rim in place to create the lid.

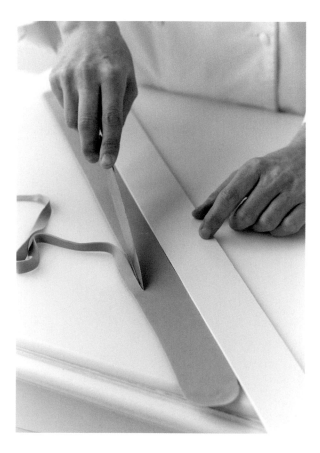

4 Photocopy each rose template (see *Templates*) three times and cut out the outer designs. Draw the roses and leaves onto the cake using pink and green edible pens. Next, cut out a second set of templates (see *Templates*), this time cutting out the roses and leaving off the leaves. Place the rose on to the cake in the same place as the other roses and mark the outlines for the petals that sit next to the leaves with pink edible pen. With the last set of templates you will need to cut out each individual petal. It's a little fiddly and you should label the pieces from 1–8 for the larger rose and a–e for the smaller rose, making sure you mark the same shapes with the same letters/numbers on your first set of templates so you know where the pieces are to be positioned.

Start with one area of the flower and continue across it, drawing around each individual petal to form the completed rose shape.

TIP

Copying the rose template a few times allows for mistakes and is useful for experimenting with the placement of the roses. If you are confident, you can just draw the petals in freehand.

5 Prepare a large glass of water for washing your brush and diluting the paste colours. Put the ruby paste food colouring onto the plate with some superwhite or white dust, keeping them separate. Mix some water and a small amount of white dust into the ruby paste food colouring to make a pale shade of pink.

6 Start painting the petals on the roses, mixing different colour strengths on your plate to gradually build up the depth of colour for each petal. The darker areas should be where the petals are furthest away from light, i.e. where they would be tucked inside another petal, and the lighter areas should be where the petals are nearest the light, i.e. towards the ends, where they open up. Try not to let the icing get too wet; if it does become wet, let it dry before continuing and use kitchen towel to dry off your brush. If you make a mistake and go too dark, simply wet your brush and wipe away most of the paste colour. Lastly, when the paste is almost dry, add the lightest colour – straight white or superwhite dust – to pick out the main highlights on the roses.

TIP

Test the strength of your colour on a piece of leftover sugarpaste (rolled fondant) in the same shade as the cake.

7 Colour the leaves in the same way using foliage green paste food colouring. Build up the colour from light to dark green then pick out the highlights with superwhite or white dust. The leaves are tucked under the rose, so make sure they are darker in those places to reflect this. When the painting is completely dry you may need to paint over it again in places, lightening and darkening the tones to bring out the design, depending on how strong you wish the pattern to be.

8 Stick the cake onto the iced base board using some royal icing. Mark two indents with the back of a paintbrush or the small end of a ball tool on either side of the cake, about 7.5mm (⅜in) down from the pink lid. Carefully move the tool around in the holes to widen them slightly so the rope can be inserted.

9 For the rope, mix enough Trex (white vegetable fat) into the caramel-coloured sugarpaste (rolled fondant) to make it soft and stretchy. Push it into the sugar gun and squeeze out as much rope as you can. Brush a little edible glue into one of the holes and stick in one end of the rope. Secure the rope against the side of the cake just below the hole to help take the weight and prevent the icing from breaking. Place the other end of the rope into the other hole, again securing it to the side of the cake. If your rope isn't long enough to reach the other side of the cake, push out another piece and neatly join them in the middle of the board.

10 To make the flower clip, roll out the caramel-coloured flower (petal/gum) paste to about 2mm (⅟₁₆in) thick. Cut out two strips, each measuring 7cm (2¾in) long and

1cm (⅜in) wide. Cut a point at one end of each strip and allow them to dry slightly. Use edible glue to secure them together, one on top of the other, and set aside.

11 Roll out the dusky pink flower (petal/gum) paste and cut out three flowers using the different size rose cutters. Bring each flower towards the end of your board and vein the petals with a veining stick, moving it back and forth over each edge to make it frill upwards. Sit each flower inside the cup of a paint palette or former for about five minutes so the outer part begins to dry then stick them together with the smallest layer on top and the largest on the outside. Sit the flower back inside the palette.

12 Cut the gold stamens so they are about 12–15mm (½–⅝in) long. Roll a pea-sized amount of the leftover dusky pink flower (petal/gum) paste into a ball. Stick the stamens into the paste one at a time and when it appears quite full; secure it into the centre of the flower using edible glue. Set the flower aside to dry completely. When dry, carefully attach the flower onto the clip part with some royal icing.

13 Stick the clip onto the cake board with royal icing then paint the clip part and the rope in gold lustre mixed with alcohol. Finish by wrapping some ribbon around the base board (see *Securing Ribbon Around Cakes and Boards*).

YOU'LL ALSO NEED

❧ 12.5cm (5in) round cake (see *Cake Recipes*), 10cm (4in) deep, iced in the same way as the main project with a pink sugarpaste (rolled fondant) band around the top (see Steps 1–3, *Romantic Rose Hatbox*)

❧ 20cm (8in) round cake board iced in pale pink sugarpaste (rolled fondant) (see *Covering Cake Boards*)

❧ Large and small rose templates (see *Templates*)

❧ Paste food colourings: claret, spruce green (Sugarflair)

❧ Dust: superwhite or white

❧ Royal icing (see *Royal Icing*)

❧ Pink edible pen

❧ 20g (¾oz) white flower (petal/gum) paste

❧ 1.5cm (¾oz) pink, double-faced satin ribbon

Simple rose hatbox

This cute mini hatbox cake is a simplified version of the main design, using an outline-only template for the main rose motif. The smaller roses are painted freehand with a simple swirl and a few petals, and the hatbox is elegantly finished with a plain rope handle.

Draw around the large rose template (see *Templates*) on top of the cake with pink edible pen. With a needle scriber, very faintly mark vertical lines about 5cm (2in) apart around the side of the cake. Use the small rose template (see *Templates*) to draw three roses at random intervals on each of the marked lines, angling each one in a different way. Use pink edible pen to draw a swirl on each of the roses, using the template as a guide.

Paint the claret colour onto the roses as for the main cake (see Steps 5–6, *Romantic Rose Hatbox*). Paint the leaves around the small roses in spruce green, setting them slightly away from the flowers and using only a few simple brushstrokes. Clean the brush and paint on the white leaves using superwhite or white dust.

When the paint is dry, secure the cake onto the base board with royal icing. Make two indents on either side about 1cm (⅜in) from the lid. Roll out the white flower (petal/gum) paste and cut a strip measuring 8mm (¼in) wide and 30cm (12in) long. Pinch each end and secure them into the indents on the cake with a small amount of edible glue. Finish by wrapping some pink ribbon around the board (see *Securing Ribbon Around Cakes and Boards*).

Vintage hat cookies

These charming cookies take classic vintage hat shapes and styles and spice them up with a more modern, fresh colour scheme that perfectly complements the main design.

To make the floppy hat, first outline the band with dusky pink royal icing and flood the area in the same colour (see *Royal-Iced Cookies*). Repeat for the stiff rimmed hat, using blue royal icing to flood. Wait about 30 minutes for the icing to dry a little then outline and flood the floppy hat cookies in blue and the stiff rim hat in white. Allow to dry for a few hours then over-pipe the details in the same colours (see *Piping with Royal Icing*).

Roll out the dusky pink flower (petal/gum) paste and cut out the blossoms using both size cutters. Frill the petals with the veining stick (see Step 11, *Romantic Rose Hatbox*) and sit them in the artist's palette to dry a little. Stick the smaller blossoms into the centre of the larger ones and return to the palette to dry completely. Colour some royal icing caramel, fill a piping bag with no.1 tube (tip) and pipe six dots into the centre of each flower. When dry, paint with the gold lustre and secure the flowers onto the cookies using royal icing.

YOU'LL ALSO NEED

❖ Cookies (see *Baking Cookies*) made using hat templates (see *Templates*)

❖ Royal icing (see *Royal Icing*)

❖ Paste food colourings: dusky pink, caramel/ivory, baby blue (Sugarflair)

❖ Dusky pink flower (petal/gum) paste

❖ Blossom cutters: 3cm (1¼in), 4cm (1½in)

❖ Veining stick

❖ Artist's palette

❖ Piping bag and no. 1 tube (tip)

❖ Gold lustre mixed with clear alcohol

SEW STYLISH

This classic sewing machine – complete with its base cabinet, black and gold colour scheme and cotton reel and lace accompaniments – instantly takes us back in time. It evokes thoughts of 1940s wartime Britain, where 'Make Do and Mend' was in full force, everything was handmade and people had to create and repair their own clothing.

The careful carving of the cake and intricate additions, such as the buttons, dials, shaped pressure foot and gold lustre details, bring the sewing machine to life. By breaking each section down into individual stages, the final impressive result becomes easily achievable.

Classic sewing machine

This traditional black and gold sewing machine is made by carefully carving cake using dowels for support, shaping with ganache and covering with black sugarpaste (rolled fondant), before adding the base boards and details.

MATERIALS

❖ One 28cm (11in) square sponge cake, 4cm (1½in) deep, made with 350g (12oz) butter etc. mix (see *Classic Sponge Cake*)

❖ One quantity of dark or white chocolate ganache (see *Ganache*)

❖ Modelling chocolate: 50g (1¾oz) dark, 20g (¾oz) white

❖ One 46 x 42cm (18 x 16½in) rectangular cake (see *Cake Recipes*), 7.5cm (3in) deep and iced in caramel-coloured sugarpaste (rolled fondant)

❖ Sugarpaste (rolled fondant): 750g (1lb 10oz) black, 30g (1⅛oz) white

❖ One 50 x 30cm (20 x 12in) rectangular cake board, covered with dark charcoal brown-coloured sugarpaste (rolled fondant) and painted (see *Icing Cake Boards*)

❖ 30 x 15cm (12 x 6in), 3mm (⅛oz) thick Australian cake board, iced 24 hours in advance in black sugarpaste (rolled fondant) so the icing also covers the sides (see *Icing Cake Boards*)

❖ Half quantity of royal icing (see *Royal Icing*)

❖ Flower (petal/gum) paste: 200g (7oz) black, 200g (7oz) caramel-coloured, 150g (5½oz) grey, 40g (1½oz) white

❖ Paste food colouring: ivory/caramel, dark brown

❖ Lustre: pearl, gold, silver

❖ Piece of 'Rose Mantilla' Sugarveil (optional) (see *Using Sugarveil*)

EQUIPMENT

❖ Two pieces of 5mm (¼in) foam board cut using two templates: A and C (see *Templates*)

❖ Paper, cut using template B (see *Templates*)

❖ Solid plastic dowel and hollow dowel, both at least 12cm (4½in) long (see *Assembling Tiered Cakes*)

❖ Circle cutters: 8cm (3¼in), 6.5cm (2⅝in), 4cm (1½in), 3.5cm (1⅜in), 2.5cm (1in), 1.5cm (⅝in) and 1cm (⅜in)

❖ Moulds: Curlicues (FPC), Filigree Brooch (FPC), Antique Buttons (FPC)

❖ Petal cutters: 1.5cm (⅝in) long, thin teardrop shape, 2.5cm (1in) long, thin petal

❖ Small piping bag (see *Making a Piping Bag*) and nos. 1, 1.5 and 4 piping tubes (tips)

❖ Sugar gun fitted with the small hole disc

❖ 1.5cm (⅝in) brown, double-faced satin ribbon

1 To make the upright arm, take the 28cm (11in) square cake and use the foam board cut from Template A (see *Templates*) to cut out three pieces of sponge as close together as possible, leaving plenty of cake for the next stage. Level the pieces and stack them up, then attach them together with ganache and trim. The height should be 10cm (4in). Take Template B and place it on the top at the back of the cake. Trim the sides, creating a slope at the front from the top to the bottom.

2 To make the horizontal arm, use a scalpel to carefully cut a slant in the underside of the foam board cut from Template C. This doesn't need to be all the way around, just at the narrowest section (see *Templates*). Cut out one piece of cake using the template then cut out a second layer using only the back two thirds of the shape. Round off the back of the shape, cut a slant down the front, then round off and carve the sides.

3 Attach the horizontal arm onto the upright arm using ganache. Measure the distance between the underside of the top piece and the workbench or board. Cut the dowels to this height. Place the hollow dowel beneath the centre of the upright arm to support it – this will be removed later. Soften the dark modelling chocolate and mould it at the top of the thin dowel for the sewing head.

TIP

Make sure the ganache is nice and soft before coating the cake, otherwise it will pull away pieces of cake rather than sealing it.

4 Using a palette knife, cover the entire machine with ganache and place it in the fridge to firm up for about 15 minutes. Soften some more dark modelling chocolate and mould it to further shape the sewing head. Cover the modelling chocolate in ganache then, if necessary, coat the entire machine in another layer of ganache to achieve a good shape. Place the cake back in the fridge for another 15 minutes to firm up again.

5 Knead about 375g (13oz) of black sugarpaste (rolled fondant) and roll out to 4mm (¼in) thick. Place the cake onto some greaseproof (wax) paper, remove the support dowel and cover the back half of the cake, using your hands to smooth the sugarpaste (rolled fondant) around the base and the back of the machine. Cut neatly around the base of the upright arm.

6 Roll out some more black sugarpaste (rolled fondant) to 4mm (¼in) thick. Cover the front section, working quickly to smooth around the top of the horizontal arm and sewing head before the sugarpaste (rolled fondant) cracks or tears. Cut it neatly where it meets the sugarpaste (rolled fondant) at the back of the machine and blend the join using your fingers. Remove any lumps where possible using a smoother.

7 Dowel the rectangular cake, iced in caramel-coloured sugarpaste (rolled fondant), using two dowels: one positioned about 6cm (2½in) from one end and the other about 18cm (7in) along from that (see *Assembling Tiered Cakes*). Secure it onto the large iced rectangular cake board using some royal icing.

8 Paint the cake and the charcoal-brown base board with dark brown paste food colouring mixed with water to make different strengths of colour. Use a flat brush and sweep back and forth over the cake to create a varnish-like effect. There is no need to paint the top of the cake or where the sewing machine will be placed.

9 Attach the thin cake board iced in black sugarpaste (rolled fondant) on top of the caramel iced cake to one end, leaving a 5mm (¼in) gap. Secure the sewing machine on to the black board using royal icing.

10 To make the balance wheel (shown below on the finished cake), roll out 20g (¾oz) of black flower (petal/ gum) paste to 3mm (⅛in) thick. Cut out a disc using the 8cm (3¼in) circle cutter and mark two circular indentations inside the disc using the 6.5cm (2⅝in) and 3.5cm (1⅜in) circle cutters. Use the 2.5cm (1in) petal/ teardrop cutter with the narrow part facing inwards to cut out eight evenly placed teardrop shapes then set aside to dry. Roll out 30g (1⅛oz) of black flower (petal/ gum) paste to 5mm (¼in) thick and cut out a disc using the 4cm (1½in) circle cutter. Set aside to dry.

11 When the discs are dry, stick the small thick one to the back of the sewing machine with some royal icing. Roll a sausage from caramel-coloured flower (petal/ gum) paste, about 4mm (¼in) in diameter and long enough to go around the balance wheel. Secure it in place with edible glue. Stick the balance wheel onto the disc at the back of the machine with royal icing. You may need to hold it in place for a minute until is secure.

12 To make the needle bar, add a tiny amount of black flower (petal/gum) paste to the white modelling chocolate and thinly roll out about half to 2mm (¹⁄₁₆in) thick and at least 6cm (2½in) long. Wrap it around the exposed dowel and trim away the excess paste at the back and the top and bottom. Blend the join with your finger. Roll a marbled-sized ball with the leftover paste then make it into a cylinder. Use a scalpel to make a lengthways slit and wrap it around the top of the covered dowel. Mould it into a cube-like shape and make it sit neatly up against the bottom of the sewing head.

13 To make the silver throat plate, thinly roll out some grey flower (petal/gum) paste, cut out a rectangle measuring 6 x 8cm (2½ x 3¼in) and round off the top. Cut out a small hole with a 1cm (⅜in) circle cutter, approximately 1.5cm (⅝in) in from the top of the rounded edge. Cut down from the bottom of the hole to the bottom of the rectangle, wrap it around the arm and tuck and stick the bottom edge under the black base board, trimming beforehand if necessary. The presser foot is made in the same way but is of course much smaller. The central piece with is cut with a scalpel and the two sides can be curled up.

14 To make the face plate that attaches to the front of the sewing head, roll out 15g (½oz) of grey flower (petal/gum) paste to a thickness of 1–2mm (1⁄16in). Cut out a rectangular piece measuring 3 x 2cm (1¼ x ¾in), rounding off the edges with a sharp knife. Use the knife to cut a slit down the centre of the piece of icing without going right to the ends and widen it slightly with the back of the knife. Attach it in place with a small amount of edible glue. Make the presser bar lifter by cutting out a tiny long teardrop shape with the 1.5cm (⅝in) cutter and cutting out a small central hole with the no. 4 piping tube (tip). Cut the pointed end flat and secure it in the gap in the plate with edible glue.

15 To make the pressure bar and upper tension buttons on top of the sewing head, on top of the needle bar and at the back of the foot, roll small balls of grey flower (petal/gum) paste in various sizes, flatten them a little and stick them together and onto the machine with edible glue. Indent a small hole into the top of the pressure bar with the end of a paintbrush.

16 Make the two dial details on the front and back sides by cutting out discs from grey flower (petal/gum) paste, approximately 3mm (⅛in) thick. Use the 1.5cm (⅝in) and 1cm (⅜in) circle cutters for the front one and the 2.5cm (1in) and 1cm (⅜in) cutters for the back one, which is also indented using the 1.5cm (⅝in) cutter.

17 The back compartment is a 4.5 x 15cm (1¾ x 6in) rectangular piece of black sugarpaste (rolled fondant) rolled out to 3–4mm (⅛in) thick, secured in place with edible glue. The knob is made from two small pieces of grey flower (petal/gum) paste, one rolled into a ball and the other into a sausage, which is then flattened.

18 To make the cotton reels, firstly make an ivory shade of flower (petal/gum) paste by mixing together 20g (¾oz) each of white and caramel-coloured flower (petal/gum) paste. Roll out to 3mm (⅛in) thick and cut out six 2.5cm (1in) round discs. Cut out three small holes from three of the discs using the no. 4 piping tube (tip). Roll three 2.5cm (1in) long cylindrical shapes from marble-sized pieces of ivory flower (petal/gum) paste and attach one end to the centre of each of the discs without holes.

19 Knead about 5ml (1 tsp) of white vegetable fat (Trex) into the white sugarpaste (rolled fondant) and 20g (¾oz) of white flower (petal/gum) paste, soften it and place into the sugar gun. Start squeezing out the paste around the cylinder of the cotton reel and work your way upwards to the top of the reel. Cut the paste at the top and repeat again if necessary. Leave a small amount of paste hanging down and attach on top of the cotton reel. Secure one reel on top of the sewing machine and the other two at the base of the cake using a tiny amount of royal icing. Roll a tiny sausage of white flower (petal/gum) paste, then form a point at one end and cut the other flat. Insert it into the hole of the cotton reel on the top of the machine.

20 Make the buttons and decorative details simply by pressing flower (petal/gum) paste into the moulds listed in the materials list and securing in place with edible glue (see *Using Moulds*). The buttons are made from white flower (petal/gum) paste dusted with pearl lustre. The decorative details on the sewing machine are made using caramel flower (petal/gum) paste. Brush gold lustre into the moulds first to help them turn out easily and to give them the traditional gold colour. Make the detail on the balance wheel by pressing paste into the brooch mould then using a 2.5cm (1in) cutter to cut out the centre only. Paint all the grey icing with silver lustre mixed with alcohol and the gold trim around the base of the machine with gold.

21 To make the piece of lace hanging at the back of the machine, use a piece of 'Rose Mantilla' Sugarveil (see *Using Sugarveil*), simply folding it to sit naturally at the back of the sewing machine.

TIP

Don't over fill the sugar gun – you need to be able to screw the top on properly.

Cotton reel mini cakes

These quirky mini cakes are a great accompaniment to the Classic Sewing Machine. They are made in a similar way to the cotton reels in the main project.

Add enough CMC (Tylose) to the pale coffee sugarpaste (rolled fondant) to make it stiff (see *Modelling Paste and CMC*) and roll it to 7mm (⅜in) thick. Cut out the top and bottom discs with an 8cm (3¼in) cutter. Use your fingers to create a slight sloping edge and cut a hole in the centre of the top piece with the 1.5cm (⅝in) cutter. Set aside for 30 minutes then secure the cake onto the bottom disc with its sloping edge facing upwards.

Mix some white vegetable fat (Trex) into the pink sugarpaste (rolled fondant) with a tiny amount of CMC (Tylose), until it becomes soft. Push it into the sugar gun and squeeze the paste out around the cotton reel, starting at the bottom. You may need to put a touch of edible glue at the base to help the pink paste stick initially. If you need to stop to refill the gun, try to join the pieces neatly.

Attach the top of the cotton reel onto the cake, with its sloped edge facing down, using edible glue or royal icing if the paste is very dry. Roll out some ivory flower (petal/gum) paste and cut out a fluted circle. Cut out a 2.5cm (1in) hole from the centre and indent with the 3cm (1¼in) circle cutter. Attach it onto the top of the cotton reel using edible glue. For the brown cotton reel, repeat using brown sugarpaste (rolled fondant).

YOU'LL ALSO NEED

❖ 5cm (2in) round miniature cakes iced thinly with pale coffee sugarpaste (rolled fondant) (see *Miniature Round Cakes*)

❖ Sugarpaste (rolled fondant): coffee, pink, medium brown

❖ Ivory flower (petal/gum) paste

❖ Circle cutters: 8cm (3¼in), 3cm (1¼in), 2.5cm (1in), 1.5cm (⅝in)

❖ Sugar gun fitted with 3mm (⅛in) hole disc

❖ 6.5cm (2⅜in) fluted round cutter

Haberdasher's cupcakes

These attractive cupcakes, featuring the lace, buttons and cotton reels from the main cake, are a haberdasher's dream. The white colour scheme would also suit a vintage bridal theme.

Carefully cut the piece of Sugarveil to sit across the cupcake – it doesn't need to cover the entire surface – and secure in place with a tiny amount of water or edible glue if necessary. Attach on the buttons and cotton reels with a small amount of royal icing.

YOU'LL ALSO NEED

❖ Cupcakes (see *Baking Cupcakes*) in silver cases, covered with pale-coffee sugarpaste (rolled fondant) discs (see *Covering Cupcakes with Sugarpaste*)

❖ Piece of Sugarveil (see *Using Sugarveil*)

❖ Buttons (see Step 20, *Classic Sewing Machine*)

❖ Cotton reels (see Steps 18–19, *Classic Sewing Machine*)

❖ Royal icing (see *Royal Icing*)

CLASSIC CRAFTING

Arts and crafts became popular in hard times when crafting became a form of entertainment. Traditional crafting is now making a comeback; people wish to take up a hobby when money is short and look to create unique items that will be cherished.

Pinwheels are traditional toys that fascinate young children and evoke thoughts of sunny days; embellishing sandcastles at the seaside and plant pots in the garden. I made my sugar pinwheels using the same methods as the paper-folded ones, using coloured sugarpaste (rolled fondant) and patterned edible papers. The button centres are quickly made with moulds and enhance the handcrafted theme.

Pretty pinwheels cake

A ribbon-embellished, pale yellow tiered cake provides the perfect backdrop for my handcrafted pinwheel embellishments. I used two different styles: a windmill and a round concertina, both of which are crafted in the same way as paper pinwheels. The edible papers add interest and decoration – either create your own to suit your colour scheme, as I have done here, or use some of the gorgeous papers found on the market.

MATERIALS

❖ One 10cm (4in) round cake, 9cm (3½in) deep; one 15cm (6in) round cake, 10cm (4in) deep; one 20cm (8in) round cake, 15cm (6in) deep; and one 25cm (10in) round cake, 12.5cm (5in) deep, each prepared and iced in pale yellow sugarpaste (rolled fondant) (see *Covering with Marzipan and Sugarpaste*)

❖ One 33cm (13in) round cake board, covered with pale yellow sugarpaste (rolled fondant) (see *Icing Cake Boards*)

❖ Flower (petal/gum) paste: 100g (3½oz) Ice Blue (Sugarflair), 80g (2⅞oz) orange, 35g (1¼oz) white, 30g (1⅛oz) red, 30g (1⅛oz) lime green, 5g (⅛oz) pale coffee, 5g (⅛oz) yellow

❖ Cornflour (optional)

❖ Quarter quantity of royal icing (see *Royal Icing*)

❖ Edible papers

EQUIPMENT

❖ 10 hollow pieces of dowel cut to size (see *Assembling Tiered Cakes*)

❖ 1.5cm (⅝in) pale coffee, grosgrain ribbon

❖ Small sharp scissors

❖ Hole punches: 3.5cm (1⅜in) round and 5cm (2in) round scallop

❖ Button mould, e.g. Plain Buttons mould (FPC)

❖ No. 1 piping tube (tip) (optional)

TIP

You can either use five different styles of edible paper or repeat the same one or two. Ensure that the hole punches are foodsafe.

1 Dowel and assemble the four tiers onto the cake board (see *Assembling Tiered Cakes*).

2 Wrap a length of 1.5cm (⅝in) grosgrain ribbon around the base of each tier and secure with double-sided tape (see *Securing Ribbon Around Cakes and Boards*).

3 For the round turquoise pinwheel, roll out just over half of the Ice Blue flower (petal/gum) paste to 1mm (1/16in) thick and cut out a 12 x 18cm (4½ x 7in) piece. Turn the paste so that its longest edge is vertical and concertina it, making 6–7mm (¼in) pleats all the way along the long side. Aim for about 13 folds in one piece.

4 When you get to the end, pinch the flower (petal/gum) paste tightly in the centre, open up the pleats on one side and secure them together with edible glue to form half of the pinwheel. Repeat to create the other half then attach the two semicircles together using edible glue. Cut out a large round scallop-edge disc from edible paper using the scallop hole punch and secure it onto the pinwheel with edible glue. Set aside to dry for a couple of hours.

TIP

Work quickly to ensure your flower (petal/gum) paste doesn't dry out or crack. You can use cornflour to prevent the paste from sticking to itself between each fold.

5 Make the orange pinwheel in the same way as the turquoise one, cutting the paste to 10 x 14cm (4 x 5½in) and folding the paste only 11 times to create larger folds. Use the round hole punch to cut out a round disc from another sheet of edible paper and attach it onto the pinwheel using edible glue.

6 To make the white windmill-style pinwheel, start by cutting out a 14.5cm (5¾in) square from a sheet of red edible paper. Roll out the white flower (petal/gum) paste to a thickness of 1mm (1⁄16in), flip it over and immediately place the edible paper onto it. It should stick without any edible glue, but if it doesn't, just use a small amount to hold it in place. Use a sharp knife to cut around the paper and cut out the paste.

7 Hold the square in your hand and make a diagonal cut from each corner, stopping about 1.5cm (1⁄16in) away from the centre.

8 Place the square back down onto the bench and fold over the paste from one corner into the centre of the pinwheel. Attach it in place with edible glue, using the end of a paintbrush to help it stick firmly down. Repeat for all four sides, sticking the points on top of each other in the centre. Set aside to dry for a couple of hours.

9 Repeat Steps 6–8 to make the other two pinwheels. One uses a 12.5cm (5in) square piece of orange edible paper and flower (petal/gum) paste and the other uses a 13.5cm (5¼in) square piece of blue edible paper and pale green flower (petal/gum) paste.

10 Make the buttons using flower (petal/gum) paste and a button mould (see *Using Moulds*). You can vary the style and shape of the buttons using different moulds. The red and orange pinwheel has a white button, the round turquoise pinwheel and blue and green pinwheel have pale coffee buttons, the white and red pinwheel has a yellow button and the round orange pinwheel has a red button.

11 Finish by attaching the pinwheels onto the cake using some royal icing, using the photograph for guidance. Finally, secure a length of grosgrain ribbon around the cake board (see *Securing Ribbon Around Cakes and Boards*).

TIP

Use a no. 1 piping tube (tip) to press out the holes on the button if the mould doesn't manage to do this.

Windmill cupcakes

These delightful cupcakes are simply styled using the handcrafted windmills from the Pretty Pinwheels Cake. Experiment with a range of paste colours and edible paper patterns to suit your occasion.

The windmill-style pinwheel toppers are made using exactly the same technique as for the *Pretty Pinwheels Cake*, using a 9cm (3½in) square of flower (petal/gum) paste and patterned edible paper in a complementary colour scheme. Simply top each cupcake with a pinwheel.

YOU'LL ALSO NEED
❖ Cupcakes (see *Baking Cupcakes*) in white paper cases, iced with a swirl of buttercream (see *Buttercream-topped Cupcakes*)

❖ Windmill-style pinwheels (see Steps 6–8, *Pretty Pinwheels Cake*)

Crafty cookie pops

Beautifully decorated with satin ribbon bows, colourful buttons and pretty edible papers, these tempting cookie pops are quick-to-make and won't be around for long! The edible papers are very simply cut using plain and scalloped-edge hole punches.

Roll out the three different colours of sugarpaste (rolled fondant) to approximately 2–3mm (⅛in) thick. Use the cutters to take out one round circle from the orange sugarpaste (rolled fondant) and two fluted circles from the other two pastes. Use edible glue to secure each one onto a cookie (see *Covering Cookies with Sugarpaste*).

Using the hole punches and patterned edible paper, cut out two plain circles for the fluted circle cookies and a scalloped-edge disc for the round orange cookie. Attach them in place with some edible glue, followed by a sugar button. Finish by tying neat ribbon bows onto the sticks, just below each cookie.

YOU'LL ALSO NEED

❖ 7.5cm (3in) round cookies baked on sticks (see *Cookie Pops*)

❖ Sugarpaste (rolled fondant): turquoise, pale yellow, orange

❖ Cutters: 7.5cm (3in) round and 6.5cm (2⅝in) fluted round

❖ Edible paper, range of styles

❖ Hole punches: 7.5cm (3in) round and 6.5cm (2⅝in) scalloped-edge

❖ Buttons: pale coffee, yellow and red (see Steps 6–8, *Pretty Pinwheels Cake*)

❖ 1.5cm (⅝in) satin ribbon in pale coffee, white and pale turquoise

TRADITIONAL TELEPHONES

The style of this traditional, rotary dial telephone is iconic of the 1930s–40s. It is perfectly suited to the Art Deco theme with its symmetrical headset, round dial and slanted sides, and reminds us how far technology has moved forward to our mobile phones today.

The classic black colour and chunky shape makes this telephone a bold object that would really stand out in the home. If you prefer something a little brighter for a special occasion, why not add a splash of colour and recreate this cake using a red sugarpaste covering to give it a more feminine touch?

Rotary dial telephone

This bold black rotary dial telephone cake really makes a statement. Its simple shape is easy to carve from cake and the headset is crafted from sugarpaste (rolled fondant). The ear and mouth pieces are cleverly made by shaping and covering polystyrene cake dummies – due to weight and gravity, these would be very difficult to form with cake! The addition of the numbered rotary dial and cord detail further add to the realism of the design.

MATERIALS

- One 18cm (7in) square cake (see *Baking Cakes*) made up of two or three layers, 10cm (4in) deep (see *Carving and Sculpting Cakes*). Alternatively, use a 35cm (14in) square cake, baked to 4cm (1½in) deep (using 600g (1lb 5oz) butter sponge mix) from which you cut out three 18 x 13.5cm (7 x 5¼in) pieces

- 500g (1lb 2oz) ganache or buttercream (see *Fillings and Coverings*)

- 30g (1⅛oz) dark or white modelling chocolate

- 1kg (2lb 4oz) black sugarpaste (rolled fondant)

- 5ml (1 tsp) CMC (Tylose) (see *Modelling Paste and CMC*)

- Flower (petal/gum) paste: 30g (1⅛oz) black, 20g (¾oz) white, 20g (¾oz) grey, 35g (1¼oz) brown

- Black edible pen

- One 30cm (12in) round cake board, covered with white sugarpaste (rolled fondant) (see *Covering Cake Boards and Dummies*)

- 45ml (3 tbsp) royal icing (see *Royal Icing*)

EQUIPMENT

- 5mm (¼in) foam board: one piece cut to 18 x 12.5cm (7 x 5in), one piece cut to 12.5 x 7.5cm (5 x 3in), one piece cut to 18 x 2cm (7 x ¾in)

- Two 5cm (2in) round, 4cm (1½in) deep polystyrene cake dummies

- Circle cutters: 8cm (3¼in), 5cm (2in) , 4cm (1½in), 3.5cm (1⅜in), 3cm (1¼in), and 1.2cm (½in)

- Two thin dowels or wooden skewers (optional) (see *Assembling Tiered Cakes*)

- 1.5cm (⅝in) oval cutter

- 1.5cm (⅝in) black with white microdot ribbon

1 Cut your 18cm (7in) square cake down one side to make it 5cm (2in) wide, unless you are cutting from a 35cm (14in cake). Sandwich the layers together with ganache or buttercream and attach the cake using more filling onto the 18 x 12.5cm (7 x 5in) foam board.

2 Make a 8cm (3¼in) mark with a small sharp knife, 9.5cm (3¾in) from the front of the cake. Repeat about 3.5cm (1⅜in) behind it. Make two slashes in-between and perpendicular to the first two and at each end. There should now be a rectangular box visible on top.

3 Using the large serrated knife, carve slopes down the front and back of the phone, falling short at both ends to create a small ledge. Carve steeper slopes down the sides of the phone. When you are happy with the shape, cover the cake in ganache or buttercream and place in the fridge to firm up for about 20 minutes.

4 Soften a marble-sized piece of dark modelling chocolate, roll into a ball then flatten slightly. Cut one side so it has a flat edge and stick it onto the rectangular top edge of the cake at one corner. Repeat this three more times for each corner to create the cradle for the handset. Roll two more marble-sized balls, mould them into rectangular pieces and position in-between the prongs on each side to enable the handset to sit up above the phone, rather than against it.

5 Cover the cake in black sugarpaste (rolled fondant) (see *Covering with Marzipan and Sugarpaste*), taking care that the icing doesn't tear, especially around the protruding prongs at the top. Ensure the sugarpaste covers and hides the base foam board.

6 Take the thin 18 x 2cm (7 x ¾in) piece of foam board and check it fits in the space for the handset, allowing for a 3–4mm (⅝in) gap on each side. Knead some CMC (Tylose) into 100g (3½oz) of black sugarpaste (rolled fondant), and set it aside to harden for a few minutes. Roll it into a sausage shape the length of the foam board, before placing it on top and moulding it into the handle shape, using smoothers to help you achieve an even shape. Set aside to harden for about an hour.

7 In the meantime, carve a dome shape into each of the polystyrene cake dummies. Carve out two flat slopes at about 45 degrees from the top of the domes – they need to be slightly wider than the width of the handle to allow for the icing once the ear and mouth pieces are covered. Check them against the underside of the handle to ensure they will fit.

8 Cover both cake dummies with black sugarpaste (rolled fondant) (see *Covering with Marzipan and Sugarpaste*). Roll out some black flower (petal/gum) paste, the length of the circumference of the iced dummies, and cut two strips measuring 1cm (⅜in) wide to fit around the bottom. Trim and secure them in place with edible glue, keeping the seam below the base of the sloped edge. Set aside to dry for a couple of hours.

9 Roll out 10g (¼oz) of white flower (petal/gum) paste and cut out an 8cm (3¼in) circle using the cutter. Set it aside to dry out a little. Roll out about 10g (¼oz) of black flower (petal/gum) paste to 2mm (¹⁄₁₆in) thick and cut out a circle in the centre using a 8cm (3¼in) cutter. Cut out the centre with the 3.5cm (1⅜in) cutter then, using the smallest 1.2cm (½in) circle cutter, cut out ten holes close to each other, beside the edge of the dial disc, leaving a gap between the first and last number hole. Roll out about 15g (½oz) of black flower (petal/gum) paste to a 4mm (⅛in) thickness and cut out a 4cm (1½in) circle.

10 Place the large black disc with the cut out number holes over the white disc and write in the numbers using a black edible pen. Lift the black dial off and secure the white dial to the cake using edible glue, followed by the 4mm (⅛in) thick, 4cm (1½in) black disc. Allow it to set for a minute or two before attaching the main dial.

TIP

You may need to hold the ear and mouth pieces in place for a few minutes, or use a support while they attach themselves.

11 Roll out a marble-sized piece of grey flower (petal/gum) paste, cut out a 3cm (1¼in) circle and secure it onto the centre of the dial. Cut a tiny oval from thinly rolled out white flower (petal/gum) paste, secure on top of the grey disc and add a squiggle on top with a black edible pen.

12 Use royal icing to secure the 12.5 x 7.5cm (5 x 3in) foam board into the centre of the prepared cake board. Secure the phone cake on top of the boards using additional royal icing. Attach the handle with royal icing, using two thin dowels or wooden skewers to support it if it feels heavy and you feel it may sink into the cake, particularly if the sponge is soft and the icing is fresh. Add a little CMC (Tylose) to some black sugarpaste (rolled fondant), roll out to a 4.5mm (¼in) thickness and cut out four rectangular pieces measuring 1.5 x 2cm (⅝ x ¾in) for the feet. Attach them to each corner under the base board using edible glue, then use royal icing to attach the ear and mouth pieces to the headset handle. Leave them to set for at least an hour.

13 To make the cord, roll all of the brown flower (petal/gum) paste into a long sausage shape, measuring 4mm (¼in) wide and at least 23cm (9in) long, using the smoother to form an even shape. Cut and attach the cord onto one end to the mouthpiece with edible glue

and push the other end underneath on the same side, towards the back of the phone. Roll another length of cord to run from underneath the back of the phone to the back edge of the cake board and cut it neatly.

14 Roll a large pea-sized amount of grey flower (petal/gum) paste into another sausage and flatten it. Cut one end and shape the other end into a blunt point. Attach using edible glue with the pointed end up over the dial between the one and the zero.

15 Thinly roll out some black flower (petal/gum) paste, cut out two 5cm (2in) circles and attach them to the underside of the ear and mouth pieces using some water or edible glue. Mix 2.5ml (½ tsp) of black sugarpaste (rolled fondant) with a small amount of water to form a paste and put it into a small piping bag. Pipe around the join of the ear and mouth pieces and the handle if there are any gaps, smoothing the paste with a damp brush as you go. Finish by securing some ribbon around the base board (see *Securing Ribbon Around Cakes and Boards*).

Retro phone cookies

These fun cookies perfectly accompany the Rotary Dial Telephone. The details are piped with royal icing and a flower (petal/gum) paste dial is used to achieve a perfectly round shape.

For the black cookie, over-pipe the outline and details using a no. 1.5 piping tube (tip) and dark grey royal icing (see *Piping with Royal Icing*). Thinly roll out some white flower (petal/gum) paste, cut out a 3cm (1¼in) circle and attach to the centre. Thinly roll out the black flower (petal/gum) paste and cut out the dial using the same cutter. Cut out ten number holes with the eyelet cutter then secure the dial in place. Cut out another tiny circle from ivory flower (petal/gum) paste, using the 1.2cm (½in) cutter. Finish by piping the small grey royal icing details on the dial with the no. 1 piping tube (tip).

Repeat to make the ivory cookie, this time using white royal icing to pipe the details, ivory flower (petal/gum) paste for the dial and adding a central black flower (petal/gum) paste circle in the centre of the dial.

YOU'LL ALSO NEED
- ❖ Shaped cookies (see *Baking Cookies*) cut with template (see *Templates*), outlined and flooded in black/ivory (see *Piping with Royal Icing*)
- ❖ Piping bag (see *Making a Piping Bag*) and no. 1 piping tube (tip)
- ❖ Royal icing: ivory, dark grey and grey (see *Royal Icing*)
- ❖ Flower (petal/gum) paste: white, ivory and black
- ❖ Circle cutters: 3cm (1¼in), 1.2cm (½in), small round eyelet cutter

Classic phone mini cake

This classic mini cake is essentially a simplified version of the Rotary Dial Telephone cake. The cream colour scheme gives it an elegant feel.

Shape the front and sides, coat and place in the fridge to firm. Cover with caramel sugarpaste (rolled fondant). Cut a 3cm (1¼in) disc from white and ivory flower (petal/gum) paste. Use the no. 4 piping tube (tip) to cut ten holes from the ivory disc then stick it onto the white disc, mark the numbers and attach. Cut a 1.2cm (½in) ivory paste disc, attach to the centre and add a caramel paste detail (see Steps 10–11, *Rotary Dial Telephone*). Roll out some more caramel paste to 2mm (¹⁄₁₆in) thick, cut a rectangle to fit the top and round off the corners. For the bells, roll two pea-sized balls, squash slightly and secure. For the cradle, cut a 4 x 0.5cm (1½ x ½in) rectangle, cut semi circles at each end and attach on the bells, lifting the ends. Leave to dry.

Roll a longer sausage shape from caramel paste, secure two tiny balls and attach on the spaghetti. Set aside for ten minutes, secure with edible glue then set aside for an hour. Roll and squash two marble-sized balls from ivory paste and stick to the spaghetti. Paint the details with diluted brown paste food colouring and gold lustre.

YOU'LL ALSO NEED

* Two layers of cake sandwiched together, cut into 5cm (2in) squares and chilled (see *Miniature Square Cakes*)
* Buttercream or ganache (see *Fillings and Coverings*)
* Light caramel-coloured sugarpaste (rolled fondant)
* Circle cutters: 3cm (1¼in), 1.2cm (½in)
* No. 4 piping tube (tip)
* Flower (petal/gum) paste: white, caramel
* Black edible pen
* Spaghetti: two 2cm (¾in) pieces
* Brown diluted paste food colouring
* Gold lustre mixed with clear alcohol

THE CHARLESTON

The Charleston became a popular jazz dance with women in the 1920s and it is now as recognized for its glamorous costumes as it is for its steps. Charleston dancers would don alluring Flapper dresses with ruffled skirts, fun feather boas and striking feathered headpieces.

I designed this tiered wedding cake to incorporate the fun and frivolity of the Charleston costume. It is certainly dressed to impress with a pretty pearl trim on the bottom tier; a layered, textured middle tier, and a top tier that represents the eye-catching Charleston headpieces with its ruffled band, floral brooch and glorious feather embellishments.

Fabulous feathers cake

Feathers add a touch of glamour and sophistication to this stylish, tiered cake. Standing proudly from the top tier and making up the layered middle tier, the feathers are all created using rice paper, giving them a softer feel than if they were formed from brittle icing. The elegant strings of sugar pearls and beautiful brooch centrepiece are so easy to create, simply by pressing flower (petal/gum) paste into moulds. Finished with a flower and ruffled band, the cake becomes a fabulously feminine showstopper that is certain to wow your guests.

MATERIALS

- ❖ One 12.5cm (5in) round cake (see *Cake Recipes*), 9cm (3½in) deep; one 18cm (7in) round cake, 15cm (6in) deep; and one 25cm (10in) round cake, 10cm (4in) deep, each prepared and iced in soft grey sugarpaste (rolled fondant) (see *Covering with Marzipan and Sugarpaste*)

- ❖ One 33cm (13in) round cake board, covered with pale grey sugarpaste (rolled fondant) (see *Icing Cake Boards*)

- ❖ Flower (petal/gum) paste: 100g (3½oz) white, 100g (3½oz) grey

- ❖ Lustre: dark silver, light silver, pearl white mixed with clear alcohol

- ❖ Silver lustre spray

- ❖ Half quantity of royal icing (see *Royal Icing*)

- ❖ Two large 75 x 40cm (30 x 16in) sheets of rice paper or equivalent

EQUIPMENT

- ❖ 7 hollow pieces of dowels cut to size (see *Assembling Tiered Cakes*)

- ❖ Rose petal cutter

- ❖ Veining stick (Jem: bark-effect)

- ❖ Apple tray, former or mould

- ❖ Moulds: Brooch (Karen Davis), Pearl (FPC)

- ❖ 2cm (¾in) circle cutter

- ❖ Scissors

- ❖ Piping Bag (see *Making a Piping Bag*)

- ❖ Feather template (see *Templates*)

- ❖ 1.5cm (⅝in) silver, double-faced satin ribbon

1 Dowel and assemble the three tiers onto the cake board (see *Assembling Tiered Cakes*).

2 Start by making the flower to allow it plenty of time to dry. Thinly roll out some white flower (petal/gum) paste and cut out five petals using the rose petal cutter. Vein the top and sides of each petal by rolling the veining stick back and forth, positioning it half on and half off the edges so they start to frill. Pop each petal into an apple tray, former or mould to dry a little.

3 Press tiny amounts of white flower (petal/gum) paste into the pearl beads in the brooch mould then fill the rest of the mould with grey flower (petal/gum) paste (see *Using Moulds*).

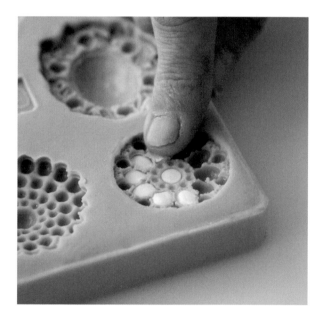

4 Roll out a small amount of white flower (petal/gum) paste and cut out a disc with the circle cutter. Dust each petal with silver lustre, using lighter silver first towards the centre of the petal and darker silver more towards the point, avoiding the frilled edge around the top of the petal. Use edible glue to secure the petals onto the white disc to form the outside of the flower, as shown.

5 Paint the brooch with silver and white pearl lustre mixed with clear alcohol. Secure it into the centre of the flower using some edible glue, or royal icing if the flower (petal/gum) paste is dry, then sit the flower into a former to dry. Paint the frilled edges of each petal with silver lustre, just catching the very ends of the edges.

TIP

It's a good idea to make more than one flower, just in case it breaks!

6 Cut strips of rice paper for the feathers around the middle tier, each measuring at least 20–25cm (8–10in) long and 8cm (3¼in) wide. Cut small triangles out from the paper all the way along each strip, with each point cut just over half way up the width of the paper. Place each strip with the smoother surface facing upwards onto a large sheet of greaseproof (wax) paper. Use a small sharp knife or scissor blade to curl the points of the paper slightly upwards.

7 Lay out a rice paper strip with its points curling upwards. Spray with silver lustre from the straight edge across to the jagged side, so the colour is weaker towards the tip of the points. Repeat for all strips. You will need one 60cm (24in) strip or two strips that make up 60cm (24in) to wrap once around, and there will be ten or eleven layers of strips to make up this tier.

8 Turn the strip over and use a piping bag to pipe a line of royal icing across the top, near the straight edge. Attach it onto the bottom of the cake using edible glue, so the points fan outwards slightly over the bottom tier. If the strip is too short to wrap all the way around, add another piece and trim them so that the two ends overlap very slightly. Add the next layer so the end is not in exactly the same place as the last piece. Continue adding pieces and making layers until you reach the top of the cake, but do not go over the top edge.

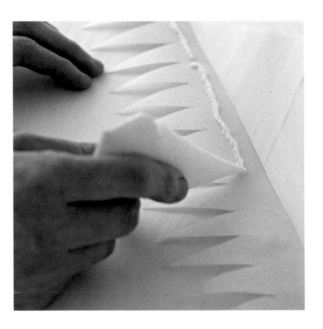

9 When you get to the top edge, cut the straight part off from the pointed strips so you are just left with the triangles. This time you need to curl the ends backwards so they sit over the edge of the cake. Stick them individually onto the cake, firstly around the top, then adding another layer right up to the top tier.

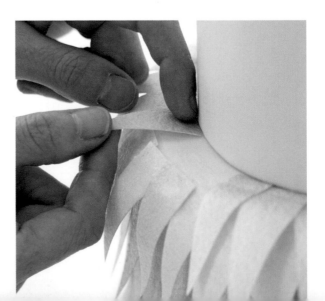

10 Thinly roll out about 40g (1½oz) of grey flower (petal/gum) paste into a long, thin strip, measuring at least 50cm (20in). Cut it to a width of 4cm (1½in) using a sharp knife. Place the strip on to a foam pad and frill and soften the two edges using a ball tool. Ruffle and fold the icing randomly, then make an indentation along the centre of the length of the strip using the back of a knife. Wrap the icing around the top tier, trim any excess and secure with edible glue so the join is at the back.

11 Cut out two rice paper feathers with scissors, using the template (see *Templates*) as a guide. Fold them in half to make a pleat, open them out and dust the centre of both feathers using the light and dark silver lustres – the colour should be stronger towards the base. Snip tiny slits on an angle all the way up both sides of each feather. Secure the smaller feather on top of the larger feather using some royal icing and part them slightly at the top. Stick them on the cake to one side using some more royal icing, then secure the sugar flower with brooch centre in front of them.

12 Brush some pearl white lustre into the pearl mould and press in some white flower (petal/gum) paste (see *Using Moulds*). Remove any excess paste, pop the pearls out and neatly stick them around the bottom tier with some edible glue. Repeat until you have enough pearls to go round the cake once then repeat again to make a second row.

13 Finish by securing some silver, double-faced ribbon around the base board (see *Securing Ribbon Around Cakes and Boards*).

Fun feather mini cakes

The rice paper feathers are the main showpiece of these glamorous mini cakes, standing proud against the crisp, white icing. The central brooch is created using a smaller mould and the trim around the base is ruffled to add extra allure.

Make the ruffle band for the base of each cake in the same way as the top tier in the main project (see Step 10, *Fabulous Feathers Cake*), just on a smaller scale. Pinch the ruffle slightly at the front. Make the feathers using the same method as for the main cake (see Step 11, *Fabulous Feathers Cake*) using the feather template (see *Templates*). Attach them onto the front of the cake, tucking the points in behind the ruffled band. Press some white flower (petal/gum) paste into the brooch mould and turn it out to dry a little. Stick it in front of the feathers using some royal icing or edible glue if the paste is still a little soft.

YOU'LL ALSO NEED

❖ 5cm (2in) round miniature cakes iced in pale grey (see *Miniature Round Cakes*)

❖ Flower (petal/gum) paste: grey, white

❖ Feather template (see *Templates*)

❖ Edible glue or royal icing

❖ Brooch mould (FPC)

Pearls and petals cupcakes

These sophisticated cupcakes adapt the flowers from the main cake to make a chic and stylish treat. The brooch centrepieces and pearl trims add a touch of class to the design.

Secure the flowers onto the cupcakes using some royal icing. Attach the soft strings of pearls around the edges of the sugarpaste (rolled fondant) with edible glue, so they sit on top of the cupcake cases, hiding the jagged edges.

YOU'LL ALSO NEED

❖ Cupcakes (see *Baking Cupcakes*) in silver cases, topped with a disc of grey sugarpaste (rolled fondant) (see *Covering Cupcakes with Sugarpaste*)

❖ Royal icing (see *Royal Icing*)

❖ Flowers with brooch centres made with 3cm (1¼in) petal cutter and smaller pearl brooch from the Jewelled Brooch mould (FPC) (see Steps 2–5, *Fabulous Feathers Cake*)

❖ White sugar pearls (see Step 12, *Fabulous Feathers Cake*)

ANTIQUE TIMEPIECES

This grand, time-honoured mantle clock would have had pride
of place on a 1930s mantelpiece. The intricate detailing, bold solid
colour and symmetrical lines and shapes are typical of the Art Deco
era from which it emerges.

This realistic piece is easier to create than you would imagine:
the fine details are drawn on with black edible pen and the lavish
embellishments are simply made using moulds. The neutral brown, gold
and ivory colour scheme is very masculine, however the design would
also suit a softer tone, such as a lighter brown or even a dusky pink.

Mantel clock masterpiece

This magnificent 1930s-style mantle clock makes a wonderful centrepiece for a male birthday or celebration. Carved layers of cake make up the shape of the clock itself, whilst the clock face and details are created from icing and the base board that lifts the cake is cleverly fashioned from covered polystyrene. The attractive detailing around the cake is created simply by using one mould in a variety ways to create a different design, whilst another mould forms the delightfully intricate draw handle.

MATERIALS

❖ One 30cm (12in) square cake, approximately 4cm (1½in) deep, baked with 450g (1lb) butter/size mix (see *Cake Recipes*)

❖ Two 12 x 8cm (4½ x 3¼in), 3mm (⅛in) deep Australian cake boards, stuck together with royal icing and covered with ivory sugarpaste (rolled fondant) (see *Icing Cake Boards*)

❖ 9 x 21.5cm (3½ x 8½in), 1cm (⅜in) foam board, iced in chocolate-flavoured or dark brown sugarpaste (rolled fondant)

❖ One quantity of ganache (see *Ganache*)

❖ 750g (1lb 10oz) chocolate flavoured or dark brown sugarpaste (rolled fondant)

❖ Flower (petal/gum) paste: 30g (1⅛oz) ivory, 10g (¼oz) mustard-coloured (made by mixing buttercup and ivory food paste), 100g (3½oz) dark brown, 15g (½oz) black, 75g (2¾oz) caramel-coloured

❖ Quarter quantity of royal icing (see *Royal Icing*)

❖ Edible black pen

❖ Gold lustre

EQUIPMENT

❖ 19 x 6 x 1.8cm (7½ x 2½ x ¾in) polystyrene

❖ 6 x 13cm (2½ x 5in) piece of 5mm (¼in) foam board

❖ 12.5cm (5in) round cake board or cutter

❖ Round cutters: 8cm (3¼in), 7cm (2¾in), 3.5cm (1⅜in), 7mm (¼in)

❖ Victorian Bauble (ornament) cutter or template (see *Templates*)

❖ Moulds: Curlicues (FPC), Filigree mould (FPC)

❖ Clock base template (see *Templates*)

❖ 1.2cm (½in) ivory/bridal white, double-faced satin ribbon

1 Moisten the sides of the polystyrene with a small amount of water and place it on to some greaseproof (wax) or silicone paper. Roll out about 200g (7oz) of chocolate-flavoured or dark brown sugarpaste (rolled fondant) to at least 18cm (7in) long and 3mm (⅛in) thick. Cut strips lengthways and use to cover the sides of the polystyrene plinth, using a sharp knife to trim away the excess and smoothers to achieve a flat surface. Secure it to the centre of the board with some royal icing then stick on the iced foam board.

2 Cut out a circle from the corner of the 30cm (12in) square cake using the 12.5cm (5in) cake board or cutter then cut it in half. Cut out three more pieces of cake, each measuring 12.5 x 6 x 11cm (5 x 2½ x 4¼in). Assemble on the foam board using ganache to secure it all together. Stick the three rectangular layers together first at the base, then sandwich the two semi-circles back to back and attach them on top of the other three layers. Cover the whole cake in ganache and place it in the fridge to firm up (see *Layering, Filling and Preparation*).

3 Roll out half of the sugarpaste (rolled fondant) to 4mm (⅛in) thick. Individually cover the front and back of the clock. Trim the paste to fit the shape once it is on the cake (see *Covering with Marzipan and Sugarpaste*). Roll out a further 350g (12oz) of sugarpaste (rolled fondant) to at least 50 x 9cm (20 x 3⅛in) and cover the sides and top of the cake again, trimming any excess paste.

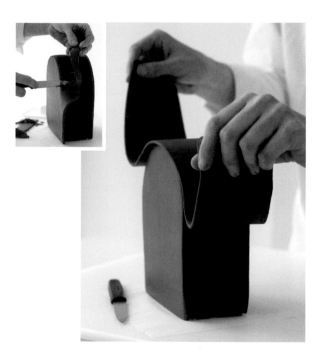

4 Use the 8cm (3¼in) cutter to cut out a circle of paste, 3cm (1¼in) down from the top of the front side of the cake.

5 Roll out the ivory flower (petal/gum) paste to 1mm (¹⁄₁₆in) thick, cut out a circle using the 8cm (3¼in) cutter and set the disc of paste aside to dry a little. Meanwhile, secure the cake onto the iced foam board base using royal icing.

6 Mix some CMC (Tylose) with 150g (5½oz) of sugarpaste (rolled fondant) until it becomes quite firm (see *Modelling Paste and CMC*). Roll the paste out to 1cm (¹⁄₁₆in) thick and cut out two shapes using either the bauble cutter or the template for the sides of the clock (see *Templates*). Cut each one in half down the centre, sandwich them back to back and secure them together with edible glue, smoothing the join to hide it as much as possible. Cut each piece flat across the bottom then set aside to dry a little, turning them over now and again. When they are stiff enough to hold their shape, stick them onto the board against the sides of the cake using edible glue.

7 Roll out 85g (3oz) of dark brown flower (petal/gum) paste to 2mm (¹⁄₁₆in) thick and 23cm (9in) long. Cut it lengthways into three strips, each one measuring 3cm (1¼in) wide. Use one strip to cut the two sides of the base board. Cut the sides to the width of the clock's

brown base board (9cm (3½in)); the height should match the distance between the ivory iced cake board and the top of the exposed foam board. Distance them 2cm (¾in) from the ivory iced cake board to the top of the foam board to hide it completely. Use the clock base template (see *Templates*) to cut out the front and back and set aside to dry until they can hold their shape. Once they are quite firm, secure the sides to the brown iced cake board, followed by the front and back pieces.

TIP

When measuring the base shape, measure the length against your own cake first, as you might need to adjust it slightly to fit.

8 To decorate the clock face, first place the 7cm (2¾in) circle cutter onto it, draw an outline with the edible black pen and mark twelve small evenly-spaced lines for each hour. Thinly roll out the mustard coloured flower (petal/gum) paste, cut out a 3.5cm (1⅜in) circle using the round cutter and attach it onto the centre of the clock face using edible glue. Neatly write in the numbers and the signature on the central disc using the edible pen.

9 Thinly roll out the black flower (petal/gum) paste and cut out the three thin hands: 2cm (¾in) long for the hour hand, 3cm (1¼in) long for the minute hand and 4.5cm (1¾in) long for the second hand. Use the small circle cutter to take out three 7mm (¼in) discs and the no. 4 piping tube (tip) to cut out two more. Secure the pieces on the clock face as shown using edible glue. Stick the 7mm (¼in) disc into the centre first followed by the hour and minute hands which sit against the centre, not on top. Next secure on the second hand going slightly across the central disc. Stick one 7mm (¼in) circle onto the hour hand towards the end and the last remaining one into the centre on top of the second hand. Finish by securing one of the tiny dots onto the minute hand and the last one into the centre of the clock face.

10 The brown detail around the outside of the clock is made using the Curlicues mould. You may need to use some Trex (white vegetable fat) to grease the mould. Press tiny amounts of dark brown flower (petal/gum) paste into the small end of the mould, pop them out and trim where the bulb detail tapers off. Use both sides of the mould and repeat until you have enough to go around the cake. Roll a small pea-sized ball with some more paste and stick it to the top centre of the clock. Attach the moulding all the way around and down both sides of the cake with edible glue.

11 The moulding around the clock face is made using only one of the scrolls in the mould. Each shape follows the next, right the way around the clock. First brush a generous amount of gold lustre into the mould (see *Using Moulds*) then press caramel-coloured flower (petal/gum) paste into the thicker, more central section of the scroll. Turn the paste out and trim it at each end. Repeat to make seven pieces in total and secure them around the clock face with edible glue.

12 To make the drawer, roll out the remaining flower (petal/gum) paste to about 3mm (⅛in) thick then cut out a 8.5 x 3cm (3⅜ x 1¼in) rectangle using a sharp knife. Secure it onto the cake with edible glue.

13 To decorate the drawer, brush some gold lustre into the diamond-like shape from the Filigree mould, then press in the caramel paste (see *Using Moulds*). Turn it out and secure it into the centre of the drawer using edible glue. From the caramel flower (petal/gum) paste, roll two tiny balls and a thin sausage shape measuring 6cm (2½in) in length. Curve the sausage around to form a handle shape then allow to dry. When it becomes quite stiff, attach it to the moulding on the drawer using edible glue and secure the two small balls at each end of the handle.

14 Finish by securing some ivory satin ribbon around the base board (see *Securing Ribbon Around Cakes and Boards*).

Antique pocket watch cupcakes

An elegant, sugarcrafted pocket watch grandly embellishes this sumptuous chocolate, buttercream-topped cupcake for a treat that people will always make time for.

Roll out a marble-sized piece of caramel-coloured flower (petal/gum) paste to 2mm (¹⁄₁₆in) thick and cut out a circle with the 4.5cm (1¾in) cutter. Thinly roll out some ivory flower (petal/gum) paste, cut out another disc with the 3.5cm (1⅜in) cutter then attach it centrally onto the caramel disc using edible glue.

   Roll out some more caramel flower (petal/gum) paste into a sausage shape measuring 15cm (6cm) long and 3mm (⅛in) thick, then trim and glue it around the clock face.

   Roll a small sausage, flatten it a little and trim it to 2.5cm (1in). Wrap it over and around the join in the paste around the top of the clock face. Roll a tiny cylindrical shape from more flower (petal/gum) paste, use the end of a paintbrush to mark to holes on either side and glue it onto the top of the watch. Draw in the details on the clock face with edible pen. Paint the caramel paste with gold lustre and set aside to dry, before placing onto the buttercream-topped cupcake.

YOU'LL ALSO NEED
* Chocolate cupcakes (see *Baking Cupcakes*) in brown foil cases and topped with a chocolate buttercream swirl (see *Buttercream-topped Cupcakes*)

* Flower (petal/gum) paste: caramel-coloured, ivory

* Edible black pen

* Circle cutters: 4.5cm (1¾in), 3.5cm (1⅜in)

* Gold lustre

Classic timepiece cookies

These magnificent pocket watch cookies stylishly echo the theme of the main cake and make a great gift for a man.

Roll out a large marble-sized piece of caramel sugarpaste (rolled fondant) to 2mm (⅛in) thick, cut out a 8cm (3¼in) circle and attach it onto the cookie using a tiny amount of water. Thinly roll out some ivory flower (petal/gum) paste, cut another disc using the 6cm (2¼in) cutter and attach. Mark on two circles using the 5.5cm (2⅛in) and 3cm (1¼in) cutters then draw in the details with edible pen.

Make the gold trim around the clock face and the top detail using the same method as for the *Antique Pocket Watch Cupcakes*. Roll a very thin, 5cm (2in) long sausage from caramel flower (petal/gum) paste, then bend it around until it starts to harden. Use edible glue to attach the two ends onto the watch so they poke into the indents. Push tissue under the ring until it is able to hold its shape.

Cut out three thin black flower (petal/gum) paste hands and a tiny central ball and attach with edible glue. Finally, paint over the caramel paste with gold lustre.

YOU'LL ALSO NEED

❖ 8cm (3¼in) round cookies (see *Baking Cookies*)

❖ Caramel-coloured sugarpaste (rolled fondant)

❖ Flower (petal/gum) paste: caramel, ivory

❖ Edible black pen

❖ Circle cutters: 8cm (3¼in), 6cm (2¼in), 5.5cm (2⅛in) and 3cm (1¼in)

❖ Gold lustre

FIFTIES DRESS

I absolutely adore the styles of 1950s women's fashion; an era that embraced femininity and celebrated the female silhouette, characterized by a full petticoat and skirt, pointed bust, small waist and rounded shoulder line. Colours were bold and embellishments came in the form of big ribbon bows, ruffled flowers, and frilly lacy sleeves.

It was such fun designing this chic red dress on a mannequin. The skirt is formed by carving and suspending cake, whilst the torso and embellishments are fashioned from icing. I love the addition of the bold ribbon bow and beautiful string of pearls – what more could a girl want!

Dressed to impress

This is one of the first cakes I have designed that needed a little construction work in its assembly! The skirt is formed from cake, which is carved on top of a shaped foam board, covered in red sugarpaste (rolled fondant) and suspended using a threaded rod, nuts and washers. The torso is simply shaped from solid modelling paste and dressed with stylish flower (petal/gum) paste decorations. The rod is cleverly disguised using modelling chocolate shaped in a dome to form a mannequin stand.

MATERIALS

* Sugarpaste (rolled fondant): 700g (1lb 9oz) very pale grey, 500g (1lb 2oz) red

* Black edible pen

* One 20cm (8in) round cake (see *Cake Recipes*), 12.5cm (5in) deep, split into/made up of three layers (see *Layering, Filling and Preparation*)

* One quantity of ganache or buttercream (see *Fillings and Coverings*)

* 100g (3½oz) dark modelling chocolate

* 145g (5¼oz) caramel/flesh-coloured modelling paste or sugarpaste (rolled fondant) with CMC (Tylose) added (see *Modelling Paste and CMC*)

* Flower (petal/gum) paste: 50g (1¾oz) red, (1¾oz) black, marble-sized piece of white

* Black paste food colouring

* White pearl lustre

* Tiny amount of clear alcohol (or Rejuvenator spirit)

EQUIPMENT

* 30cm (12in) round cake drum

* Drill

* 22cm (8½in) threaded 1cm (⅜in) diameter rod

* 3 nuts, 3 washers: 4cm (1½in) in diameter, all to fit the 1cm (⅜in) diameter rod

* 7.5mm (¼in) circle cutter

* 30cm (12in) round disc, cut from 1cm (⅜in) foam board (to fit under the cake drum)

* Glue gun or strong glue

* 5mm (¼in) foam board cut in the shape of the dress template (see *Templates*)

* Wooden skewer

* 12.5 or 15cm (5 or 6in) round cake dummy

* 1 piece of hollow dowel cut to size (see *Assembling Tiered Cakes*)

* 2.5cm (1in) red satin ribbon

* 1.5cm (⅝in) black with white polka dot ribbon

1 Drill a 1cm (⅜in) hole in the centre of the 30cm (12in) round cake drum. Insert one end of the threaded rod until it comes through by 7mm (¼in) on the underside. Pop a washer on both sides of the drum followed by two nuts and tighten them to firmly to fix the rod to the drum. Thread the third nut over the rod until it is approximately 9.5cm (3¼in) from the base board then slip over the last washer.

2 Use an edible pen to draw around the circle cutter in the centre of the 30cm (12in) round foam board then cut out the hole using a scalpel. Heat the glue gun and stick the foam board under the cake drum. If the foam board sticks out a little further than the drum, shave any excess off with the scalpel so the two boards sit flush together.

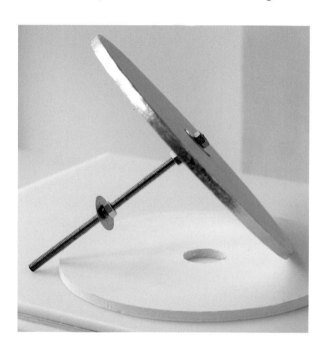

TIP

When using the glue gun, you will need to work quickly before the glue starts to set.

3 Roll out the pale grey sugarpaste (rolled fondant) to approximately 4mm (⅛in) thick, trying to maintain a circular shape. Cut a slit from the centre of the icing out to one edge then carefully move the icing onto the drum and around the central pole. Quickly join the sugarpaste (rolled fondant) back together at the slit, blending it with your fingers, then smooth it and finish off covering the board (see *Icing Cake Boards*).

4 Use a metal ruler to mark five parallel grooves at equal distances apart in the sugarpaste (rolled fondant) across the board. When you reach the centre of the board, you will need to mark the groove on either side of the pole. Set aside to dry for a couple of hours.

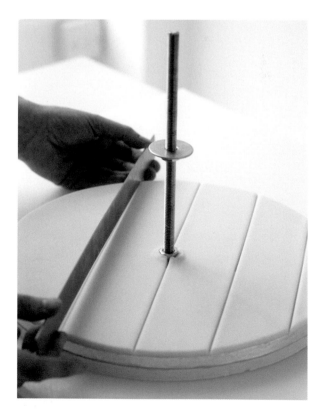

5 Cut a small central hole in the shaped 5mm (¼in) foam board using a scalpel. It needs to be at least 1cm (⅜in), but not much bigger, so the rod just fits through. Attach the three layers of cake on top of one another with a thin layer of ganache or buttercream. Stick the foam board on top with ganache/buttercream and insert the skewer into the layered cake through the hole. Turn it upside down onto the dummy and stick the skewer down through the cake, into the dummy to keep it still.

6 Gradually start carving the shape of the dress using a large serrated knife. The top of the skirt should almost come to a point where the torso begins. As the dress starts to take on more shape, carve pleats where the foam board template goes inwards. Continue to carve until you come right up against the foam board.

7 Soften small amounts of modelling chocolate and squash pieces onto the foam board at the base of the skirt to create a continuous border around the pleats. Use a palette knife to cover the whole skirt in ganache or buttercream (see *Ganache*). Place the cake in the fridge for a short while to firm up.

TIP

If you are transporting the cake, it is best to completely finish decorating it whilst it is still on the dummy and then carefully place it onto the stand at the venue.

8 Remove the cake from the fridge. Roll out the red sugarpaste (rolled fondant) to 4mm (⅛in) thick and cover the dress, allowing the icing to hang down the sides. Using a scalpel or sharp knife, cut around the sugarpaste (rolled fondant), just below the base. Use your fingers to slightly lift up and shape the sugarpaste (rolled fondant) here and there, to give the skirt some movement.

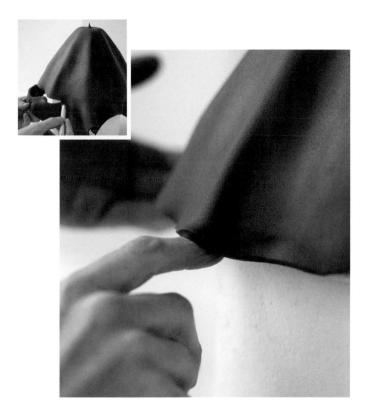

9 To make the torso, start by rolling all of the caramel/flesh-coloured modelling paste into a ball. Squeeze a little at one end, using the base of your hand to create the waist then use the work surface to create the flat base at the bottom of the torso. Squeeze again more firmly at the other end to make the neck and flatten slightly to make the shoulders, before carefully pulling out the arms and bust. Work fairly quickly to get the initial shape before the paste dries out and cracks. Once you have achieved this, carefully smooth it with your fingers until you are happy with the final shape. Cut the neck flat at the top with a small sharp knife then sit the torso aside to dry a little.

10 Heavily dilute a small amount of black food paste colouring with water and brush it over the iced cake board using a flat paintbrush. Try not to make the icing too wet and ensure you get enough colour into the grooves on the board to make them look quite dark.

11 Tightly but thinly wrap clingfilm (plastic wrap) over the top of the rod, down as far as the nut and washer. Remove the skewer and measure and cut a hollow dowel to sit inside the skirt. Lift the cake off the dummy and very carefully lower it over the stand so the wrapped metal rod goes through the hole in the foam board and into the hollow dowel in the cake.

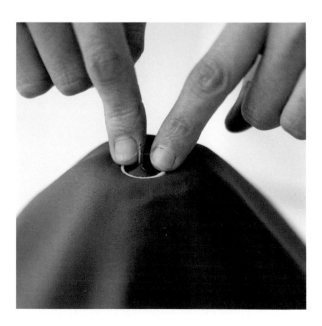

12 Stick the torso onto the skirt using edible glue. Thinly roll out approximately 25g (1oz) of red flower (petal/gum) paste into a 5cm (2in) wide strip. Cut a 'v' in the centre and curve it outwards on each side to cover the bust. You will need to pick the icing up and keep checking it against the torso to make sure that it fits the shape of the bust.

13 Wrap the ends around the back of the torso, trim them to fit together and secure in place with edible glue. You may also need to trim the sugarpaste (rolled fondant) at the base, around the waistline, so it doesn't overlap too much with the skirt.

TIP

Stick a cocktail stick between the skirt and the torso to help to secure the torso in place.

14 Thinly roll out 20g (¾oz) of black flower (petal/gum) paste to 10cm (4in) in length and cut out three or four 7mm (¼in) wide strips. Wrap one strip around the waist, trim and secure in place with edible glue. For the bow, take another black flower (petal/gum) paste strip and cut it to about 7cm (2¾in) in length. Pinch it in the middle and at both ends, then fold the ends inwards into the middle and attach in place with a little edible glue. Cut a 2.5cm (1in) strip and wrap and secure it around the centre of the bow. Cut two more pieces measuring 7cm (2¾in) long for the tails, pinch them at one end and stick them together onto the black band on one side of the dress. Cut the tails diagonally at an angle.

15 Thinly roll out the leftover black flower (petal/gum) paste into a long thin strip and cut out pieces to any length, approximately 1.5cm (⅝in) wide. Frill one side using a ball tool and foam pad then carefully attach the pieces with edible glue onto the base of the underside of the skirt to make the frilled edge hang out slightly below the hem of the red dress.

16 Cut a small strip of black flower (petal/gum) paste to run down the back of the dress. Secure four buttons made with tiny red sugarpaste (rolled fondant) balls in place using a very small amount of edible glue.

17 To cover the metal at the base of the stand, thinly roll out a marble-sized piece of dark modelling chocolate to the length of the distance between the exposed nut on the iced drum and the underside of the dress. Cut the width to 3cm (1¼in) and wrap it around the rod, joining it at the back. Trim the excess with a scalpel and blend the cut together by rubbing it with your fingers.

18 To form the dome shape for the base of the stand, roll a 40g (1½oz) ball from dark modelling chocolate and flatten it on your work surface. Make one straight cut from the centre to the outside then wrap it around the covered pole, again positioning the seam at the back. Blend the cut and reshape the dome if necessary when in place.

19 For the top of the stand, roll a large pea-sized ball from the modelling chocolate, squash it flat and attach it to the top of the neck. Roll another tiny amount of modelling chocolate into a ball, form a cone shape making the end flat instead of pointed and secure it onto the top.

20 To make the pearl necklace, roll about 25 tiny balls from white flower (petal/gum) paste, each measuring about 1–2mm (⅟₁₆in) in diameter. Secure in place with edible glue then paint with lustre. Secure a length of red ribbon and black and white polka dot ribbon around the base board (see *Securing Ribbon Around Cakes and Boards*).

Little black dress

This little black dress mini cake is a chic alternative to the main design, beautifully embellished with a red ribbon bow and clothes hanger. Carve the skirt in the same way as the Dressed to Impress cake, this time making the top part from thin pieces of flower (petal/gum) paste.

Sandwich together the two cake layers with ganache or buttercream. Use a small, serrated knife to carve the skirt shape, cutting in pleats for a natural look (see Step 6, *Dressed to Impress*). The top should have a flat, slightly oval shape. Coat the outside in ganache or buttercream and refrigerate briefly before covering with black sugarpaste (rolled fondant).

Roll a marble-sized black sugarpaste (rolled fondant) ball and secure it to the top of the cake with edible glue. Flatten the ball slightly and mould it to continue the shape of the waistline. Roll out more black paste and use the template as a guide to cut out the front and back, adjusting the template as necessary to suit the size and shape of your cake. Stick the front and back around the sugarpaste (rolled fondant) ball and secure the sides together, leaving the top.

For the sleeves, use the template or cut two small rectangles, curving one side on each sleeve. Fold the pieces in half, stick with edible glue and secure in place, slipping them inside where the sides meet. Allow to dry. Roll a very thin sausage shape with brown flower (petal/gum) paste and allow to harden a little. When nearly dry, glue each end into the sleeves. Roll a small ball and hook from grey sugarpaste (rolled fondant) and secure onto the hanger with edible glue.

Stylish dress cookies

Unleash your inner fashion designer and have fun creating pretty dress designs in cookie form. You can easily experiment with different styles using the same cutter and adjusting the shape at the neck and shoulder line by cutting out more dough after the initial cut.

Outline and flood your cookies (see *Run-out Icing*) with white or coloured red royal icing. 'Drop-in' dots (see *Piping with Royal Icing*) for a spotty dress effect. Overpipe the seam details with a no.1 piping tube (tip) once the icing is dry. Cut collars and bows with a sharp knife from black flower (petal/gum) paste and the small flower with a blossom cutter. Secure in position on the dresses with edible glue.

YOU'LL ALSO NEED

❖ Cookies (see *Baking Cookies*) cut out using Fancy dress copper cookie cutter, then cut again freehand

❖ Royal icing (see *Royal Icing*)

❖ Red paste food colouring

❖ Black flower (petal/gum) paste

❖ Small blossom cutter

❖ Piping bag and no. 1 piping tube (tip)

Recipes and Techniques

CAKE RECIPES

You want your cakes to taste delicious as well as look fabulous so always source the best-quality ingredients to ensure a superior flavour. Bake your cake in a tin that is 2.5cm (1in) larger than the required final dimensions to achieve a professional, crust-free finish every time. The sizes and quantities specified in the charts that follow in this section will make cakes about 9cm (3½in) deep. For shallower cakes and mini cakes, use smaller quantities (see *Mini Cakes*).

Measuring in cups

If you prefer to use US cup measurements, please use the following conversions:

Liquid

1 tsp = 5ml
1 tbsp = 15ml (or 20ml for Australia)
 cup = 120ml/4fl oz
1 cup = 240ml/8fl oz

Caster (superfine) sugar/brown sugar

 cup = 100g/3oz
1 cup = 200g/7oz

Butter

1 tbsp = 15g/oz
2 tbsp = 25g/1oz
 cup/1 stick = 115g/4oz
1 cup/2 sticks = 225g/8oz

Icing (confectioners') sugar

1 cup = 115g/4oz

Flour

1 cup = 125g/4oz

Sultanas (golden raisins)

165g/5oz

PREPARING CAKE TINS

It is important to take the time to line the bottom and sides of your cake tin (pan) properly before adding the cake mixture and baking it. This will prevent your cake from sticking.

1 Grease the inside of the tin with a little melted butter or sunflower oil spray to help the paper to stick and sit securely in the tin without curling up.

2 For round cakes, to line the bottom, lay your tin on a piece of greaseproof (wax) paper or baking (parchment) paper and draw around it using an edible pen. Using scissors, cut on the inside of the line so that the circle will be a good fit and put aside. Cut a long strip of the paper at least 9cm (3in) wide, fold over one of the long sides by about 1cm (⅜in) and crease firmly, then open out. Cut slits from the edge nearest to the fold

up to the fold 2.5cm (1in) apart. Put the strip around the inside of tin, with the fold tucked into the bottom corner, then add the circle and smooth down.

3 For square cakes, lay a piece of greaseproof or baking paper over the top of the tin. Cut a square that overlaps it on each side by 7.5cm (3in). Cut a slit at each end on two opposite sides. Push the paper inside the tin and fold in the flaps.

Cake portion guide

The following chart indicates about how many portions the different sizes of cake will make. The number of portions specified is based on each piece of cake being about 2.5cm (1in) square and 9cm (3½in) deep. As fruit cake is much richer, you may consider allowing for smaller portions.

Size	10cm (4in)		13cm (5in)		15cm (6in)		18cm (7in)		20cm (8in)		23cm (9in)		25cm (10in)		28cm (11in)	
Shape	O	Sq	O	Sq	O	Sq	O	Sq	O	Sq	O	Sq	O	Sq	O	Sq
Portions	5	10	10	15	20	25	30	40	40	50	50	65	65	85	85	100

CLASSIC SPONGE CAKE

For a really light sponge cake, separate the mixture between two tins for optimum results. If you want to make three layers of cake, split the mixture one-third/two-thirds. For smaller cakes, you can also cut three layers of sponge from a larger square cake. For example, a 15cm (6in) round cake can be cut from a 30cm (12in) square cake (see *Note* (above chart) and also *Layering, Filling and Preparation*).

TIP

Ensure that your butter and eggs are at room temperature before you start.

1 Preheat your oven to 160°C/325°F/Gas Mark 3 and line your tins (pans) (see *Preparing Cake Tins*).

2 In a large electric mixer, beat the butter and sugar together until light and fluffy. Add the eggs gradually, beating well between each addition, then add the flavouring.

3 Sift the flour, add to the mixture and mix very carefully until just combined.

4 Remove the bowl from the mixer and fold the mixture through gently with a spatula to finish. Tip the mixture into your prepared tin or tins and spread with a palette knife or the back of a spoon.

5 Bake in the oven until a skewer inserted into the centre of your cakes comes out clean. The baking time will vary depending on your oven. Check small cakes after 20 minutes and larger cakes after 40 minutes.

6 Leave to cool, then wrap the cake well in cling film (plastic wrap) and refrigerate until ready to use.

Deeper cakes

For deeper cakes, simply bake up to one and a half times the recipe. You may need to do this in two batches if you only have a couple of tins. Leave the cakes to cool slightly before turning them out and refilling the tins with the mixture.

Shelf life

Sponges should be made up to 24 hours in advance. Freeze the sponges if they are not being used the next day. After the 1–2-day process of layering and covering the cakes, the finished cakes should last up to 3–4 days out of the fridge.

Note: If cutting three layers from a larger square cake: for a 15cm (6in) round cake, bake an 8-egg/400g (14oz) butter etc. mix in a 30cm (12in) square tin; for a 13cm (5in) round or square cake, bake a 7-egg/350g (12oz) mix in a 28cm (11in) square tin; for a 10cm (4in) round or square cake, bake a 6-egg/300g (10oz) mix in a 25cm (10in) square tin. Add 5–10 per cent extra flour for deeper tiers or if you find that your sponges are too soft to work with.

Cake size round square	13cm (5in) 10cm (4in)	15cm (6in) 13cm (5in)	18cm (7in) 15cm (6in)	20cm (8in) 18cm (7in)	23cm (9in) 20cm (8in)	25cm (10in) 23cm (9in)	28cm (11in) 25cm (10in)	30cm (12in) 28cm (11in)
Unsalted butter	150g (5½oz)	200g (7oz)	250g (9oz)	325g (11½oz)	450g (1lb)	525g (1lb 3oz)	625g (1lb 6oz)	800g (1lb 12oz)
Caster (superfine) sugar	150g (5½oz)	200g (7oz)	250g (9oz)	325g (11½oz)	450g (1lb)	525g (1lb 3oz)	625g (1lb 6oz)	800g (1lb 12oz)
Medium eggs	3	4	5	6	9	10	12	14
Vanilla extract (tsp)	½	1	1	1½	2	2	2½	4
Self-raising (-rising) flour	150g (5½oz)	200g (7oz)	250g (9oz)	325g (11½oz)	450g (1lb)	525g (1lb 3oz)	625g (1lb 6oz)	800g (1lb 12oz)

Additional flavourings

Lemon Add the finely grated zest of one lemon per 100g (3oz) sugar.
Orange Add the finely grated zest of two oranges per 250g (9oz) sugar.
Chocolate Replace 15g (½oz) flour with 15g (½oz) cocoa powder (unsweetened cocoa) per 100g (3oz) flour.
Banana Replace the caster (superfine) sugar with brown sugar. Add 1 mashed overripe banana and 1 tsp mixed spice (apple pie spice) per 100g (3oz) flour.
Coffee and walnut Replace 15g (½oz) flour with 15g (½oz) finely chopped walnuts per 100g (3oz) flour. Replace the caster (superfine) sugar with brown sugar and add cooled shots of espresso coffee to taste.

CLASSIC CHOCOLATE CAKE

This recipe makes a chocolate cake with a wonderfully light texture, and it's also quick and easy. Make sure you split the mixture between two tins, dividing it equally or, for a three-layered cake, into one-third and two-thirds. For a really sumptuous result, fill with ganache rather than buttercream (see *Fillings and Coverings*).

1 Preheat your oven to 160°C/325°F/Gas Mark 3 and line your tins (pans) (see *Preparing Cake Tins*).

2 Sift the flour, cocoa and baking powder together.

3 In a large electric mixer, beat the butter and sugar together until light and fluffy. Meanwhile, crack your eggs into a separate bowl.

4 Add the eggs to the mixture gradually, beating well between each addition.

5 Add half the dry ingredients and mix until just combined before adding half the milk. Repeat with the remaining ingredients. Mix until the mixture starts to come together.

6 Finish mixing the ingredients together by hand with a spatula, and spoon into your prepared tins.

7 Bake in the oven until a skewer inserted into the centre of your cakes comes out clean. The baking time will vary depending on your oven. Check smaller cakes after 20 minutes and larger cakes after 40 minutes.

8 Leave to cool, then wrap the cakes well in cling film (plastic wrap) and refrigerate until ready to use.

Deeper cakes

For deeper cakes, simply bake up to one and a half times the recipe. You may need to do this in two batches if you only have a couple of tins. Leave the cakes to cool slightly before turning them out and refilling the tins with the mixture.

Shelf life

Chocolate cakes should be made up to 24 hours in advance. Freeze the cakes if they are not being used the next day. After the 1–2-day process of layering and covering the cakes, the finished chocolate cakes should last up to 3–4 days out of the fridge.

Cake size								
round	13cm (5in)	15cm (6in)	18cm (7in)	20cm (8in)	23cm (9in)	25cm (10in)	28cm (11in)	30cm (12in)
square	10cm (4in)	13cm (5in)	15cm (6in)	18cm (7in)	20cm (8in)	23cm (9in)	25cm (10in)	28cm (11in)
Plain (all-purpose) **flour**	170g (6oz)	225g (8oz)	280g (10oz)	365g (12½oz)	500g (1lb 2oz)	585g (1lb 4½oz)	700g (1lb 9oz)	825g (1lb 13oz)
Cocoa powder (unsweetened cocoa)	30g (1oz)	40g (1½oz)	50g (1¾oz)	65g (2¼oz)	90g (3¼oz)	100g (3½oz)	125g (4½oz)	150g (5½oz)
Baking powder (tsp)	1½	2	2½	3¼	4½	5¼	6¼	7½
Unsalted butter	150g (5½oz)	200g (7oz)	250g (9oz)	325g (11½oz)	450g (1lb)	525g (1lb 3oz)	625g (1lb 6oz)	750g (1lb 10oz)
Caster (superfine) **sugar**	130g (4½oz)	175g (6oz)	220g (8oz)	285g (10oz)	400g (14oz)	460g (1lb)	550g (1lb 4oz)	650g (1lb 7oz)
Large eggs	2½	3	4	5	7	8½	10	12
Full-fat (whole) **milk**	100ml (3½fl oz)	135ml (4½fl oz)	170ml (5¾fl oz)	220ml (7¾fl oz)	300ml (10fl oz)	350ml (12fl oz)	425ml (15fl oz)	500ml (18fl oz)

Additional flavourings

Orange Use the finely grated zest of 1 orange per 2 eggs.

Coffee liqueur Add 1 cooled shot of espresso coffee per 2–3 eggs and add coffee liqueur to taste to the sugar syrup (see *Fillings and Coverings*).

Chocolate hazelnut Replace 10 per cent of the flour with the same quantity of ground hazelnuts and layer with chocolate hazelnut spread and ganache (see *Fillings and Coverings*).

CARROT CAKE

The addition of chopped pecans to this carrot cake mixture not only brings an extra dimension of flavour but adds great texture too. I would recommend sandwiching together two layers only with a single layer of buttercream to make one tier, in which case you need to divide the cake mixture between two tins for baking. For a perfect flavour combination, choose lemon-flavoured buttercream for the filling (see *Fillings and Coverings*).

1 Preheat your oven to 160°C/325°F/Gas Mark 3 and line your tins (pans) (see *Preparing Cake Tins*).

2 In a large electric mixer, beat together the sugar and vegetable oil for about 1 minute or until the ingredients are well combined.

3 Crack your eggs into a separate bowl and add them to the mixture one at a time, beating well between each addition.

4 Sift together the dry ingredients and add them to the cake mixture, alternating with the grated carrot.

5 Fold in the chopped pecans.

6 Divide the mixture between the two prepared tins and bake in the oven for 20–50 minutes, depending on size. Check that the cakes are cooked by inserting a skewer into the centre, which should come out clean.

7 Leave to cool, then wrap the cakes well in cling film (plastic wrap) and refrigerate until ready to use.

TIP

You can replace the pecans with walnuts, hazelnuts or a mixture of nuts, if you prefer.

Deeper cakes

For deeper cakes, simply bake up to one and a half times the recipe. You may need to do this in two batches if you only have a couple of tins. Leave the cakes to cool slightly before turning them out and refilling the tins with the mixture.

Shelf life

Carrot cakes should be made up to 24 hours in advance. Freeze the cakes if they are not being used the next day. After the 1–2-day process of layering and covering the cakes, the finished cakes should last up to 3–4 days out of the fridge.

Cake size								
round	13cm (5in)	15cm (6in)	18cm (7in)	20cm (8in)	23cm (9in)	25cm (10in)	28cm (11in)	30cm (12in)
square	10cm (4in)	13cm (5in)	15cm (6in)	18cm (7in)	20cm (8in)	23cm (9in)	25cm (10in)	28cm (11in)
Brown sugar	135g (4½oz)	180g (6oz)	250g (9oz)	320g (11oz)	385g (13½oz)	525g (1lb 3oz)	560g (1lb 4oz)	735g (1lb 9½oz)
Vegetable oil	135ml (4½fl oz)	180ml (6fl oz)	250ml (9fl oz)	320ml (11fl oz)	385ml (13½fl oz)	525ml (18½fl oz)	560ml (19fl oz)	735ml (25fl oz)
Medium eggs	2	2½	3	4	5	6½	7	9
Self-raising (-rising) flour	200g (7oz)	275g (9½oz)	375g (13oz)	480g (1lb 1oz)	590g (1lb 5oz)	775g (1lb 11oz)	850g (1lb 14oz)	1.1kg (2lb 7oz)
Mixed spice (apple pie spice) **(tbsp)**	1	1½	2	2½	3	4	4½	5½
Bicarbonate of soda (baking soda) **(tsp)**	¼	½	¾	¾	1	1	1¼	1½
Finely grated carrot	300g (10½oz)	385g (13½oz)	525g (1lb 3oz)	675g (1lb 8oz)	825g (1lb 13oz)	1.05kg (2lb 5oz)	1.2kg (2lb 10½oz)	1.5kg (3lb 5oz)
Finely chopped pecans	65g (2¼oz)	85g (3oz)	120g (4¼oz)	150g (5½oz)	175g (6oz)	240g (8½oz)	270g (9½oz)	350g (12oz)

TRADITIONAL FRUIT CAKE

After many years of trying different fruit cake recipes, this one is a firm favourite. You can vary the types of dried fruit used or, for convenience, use a pack of ready-mixed dried fruit. My choice of alcohol for flavouring is a mix of equal quantities cherry and regular brandy, but you can use rum, sherry or whisky instead if you prefer. Soak your dried fruit and mixed candied peel in the alcohol for at least 24 hours beforehand. For the best results, leave the baked cake to mature for at least 1 month before serving. During the storage time, you can 'feed' your cake with your chosen alcohol once every week or two to improve the flavour still further and keep it really moist. For an even coating, use a spray bottle to spray the alcohol over the surface. Leave to soak in for 1–2 minutes, then rewrap.

1 Preheat your oven to 150°C/300°F/Gas Mark 2 and line your tin (pan) with two layers of greaseproof (wax) paper or baking (parchment) paper for small cakes, and three layers for larger cakes (see *Preparing Cake Tins*).

2 In a large electric mixer, beat the butter and sugar together with the lemon and orange zest until fairly light and fluffy. Add the orange juice to the soaked fruit and mixed candied peel.

3 Gradually add your eggs, one at a time, beating well between each addition.

4 Sift the flour and spices together and add half the flour mixture together with half the soaked fruit mixture to the cake mixture. Mix until just combined and then add the remaining flour mixture and fruit mixture.

5 Gently fold in the ground almonds and treacle with a large metal spoon until all the ingredients are combined and then spoon the mixture into your prepared baking tin.

6 Cover the top loosely with some more greaseproof or baking paper and then bake in the oven for the time indicated or until a skewer inserted into the centre comes out clean.

7 Pour some more alcohol over the cake while it's still hot and leave to cool in the tin.

8 Remove from the tin and wrap your cake in a layer of greaseproof paper and then foil to store.

Deeper cakes
Unfortunately, fruit cakes can't be made any bigger than the height of the tin. If you need to give your fruit cake a little extra height, you can double-board it (place it on two cake boards stuck together with royal icing) or add a thicker layer of marzipan to the top of the cake before icing it. All fruit cakes are covered with marzipan before being iced.

Shelf life
Fruit cakes should be made at least 4–6 weeks before being served to allow enough time for them to mature. They can be stored for up to 9 months or frozen to further preserve their shelf life.

Cake size round / square	10cm (4in) 10cm (4in)	13cm (5in) 10cm (4in)	15cm (6in) 13cm (5in)	18cm (7in) 15cm (6in)	20cm (8in) 18cm (7in)	23cm (9in) 20cm (8in)	25cm (10in) 23cm (9in)	28cm (11in) 25cm (10in)	30cm (12in) 28cm (11in)
Currants	100g (3½oz)	125g (4½oz)	175g (6oz)	225g (8oz)	300g (10½oz)	375g (13oz)	450g (1lb)	550g (1lb 4oz)	660g (1lb 7½oz)
Raisins	125g (4½oz)	150g (5½oz)	200g (7oz)	275g (9½oz)	350g (12oz)	450g (1lb)	555g (1lb 4oz)	675g (1lb 8oz)	800g (1lb 12oz)
Sultanas (golden raisins)	125g (4½oz)	150g (5½oz)	200g (7oz)	275g (9½oz)	350g (12oz)	450g (1lb)	555g (1lb 4oz)	675g (1lb 8oz)	800g (1lb 12oz)
Glacé (candied) **cherries**	40g (1½oz)	50g (1¾oz)	70g (2½oz)	100g (3½oz)	125g (4½oz)	150g (5½oz)	180g (6oz)	200g (7oz)	250g (9oz)
Mixed candied peel	25g (1oz)	30g (1oz)	45g (1½oz)	50g (1¾oz)	70g (2½oz)	85g (3oz)	110g (4oz)	125g (4½oz)	150g (5½oz)
Cherry brandy & brandy mix (tbsp)	2	2½	3	3½	5	6	7	8	9
Slightly salted butter	100g (3½oz)	125g (4½oz)	175g (6oz)	225g (8oz)	350g (12oz)	375g (13oz)	450g (1lb)	550g (1lb 4oz)	660g (1lb 7½oz)
Brown sugar	100g (3½oz)	125g (4½oz)	175g (6oz)	225g (8oz)	350g (12oz)	375g (13oz)	450g (1lb)	550g (1lb 4oz)	660g (1lb 7½oz)
Grated zest of lemon (per fruit)	¼	½	¾	1	1½	2	2	2½	3
Grated zest of small orange (per fruit)	¼	½	¾	1	1½	2	2	2½	3
Juice of small orange (per fruit)	¼	¼	½	½	¾	¾	1	1½	1½
Medium eggs	2	2½	3	4½	6	7	8½	10	12
Plain (all-purpose) **flour**	100g (3½oz)	125g (4½oz)	175g (6oz)	225g (8oz)	350g (12oz)	375g (13oz)	450g (1lb)	550g (1lb 4oz)	660g (1lb 7½oz)
Mixed spice (apple pie spice) (tsp)	½	½	¾	¾	1	1¼	1½	1½	1¾
Ground nutmeg (tsp)	¼	¼	½	½	½	¾	¾	1	1
Ground almonds	10g (¼oz)	15g (½oz)	20g (¾oz)	25g (1oz)	35g (1¼oz)	45g (1½oz)	55g (2oz)	65g (2¼oz)	75g (2¾oz)
Flaked (slivered) **almonds**	10g (¼oz)	15g (½oz)	20g (¾oz)	25g (1oz)	35g (1¼oz)	45g (1½oz)	55g (2oz)	65g (2¼oz)	75g (2¾oz)
Black treacle (blackstrap molasses) (tbsp)	½	¾	1	1½	1½	1¾	2	2½	3
Baking time (hours)	2½	2¾	3	3½	4	4½	4¾	5½	6

FILLINGS AND COVERINGS

Fillings are used to add extra flavour and moisture to a cake, and the choice of filling should complement the type or flavour of the sponge. The most popular and versatile fillings are buttercream and ganache, with ganache generally used for chocolate-covered cakes. These recipes can be safely used on cakes displayed at room temperature, avoiding the need to refrigerate them until ready to serve. Fillings are also used to seal and coat the cake, cover over any gaps, correct any imperfections and create a firm, smooth surface for the icing.

BUTTERCREAM (FROSTING)

Makes about 500g (1lb 1oz); enough for an 18–20cm (7–8in) round or square layer cake, or 20–24 cupcakes.

MATERIALS

❖ 170g (6oz) unsalted or slightly salted butter, softened

❖ 340g (12oz) icing (confectioners') sugar

❖ 2 tbsp (30ml) water

❖ 1 tsp (5ml) vanilla extract or alternative flavouring

EQUIPMENT

❖ Large electric mixer

❖ Spatula

1 Put the butter and icing (confectioners') sugar in the bowl of a large electric mixer and mix, starting on a low speed to prevent the mixture from going everywhere.

2 Add the water and vanilla or other flavouring and increase the speed, beating the buttercream really well until it is pale, light and fluffy.

3 Store in an airtight container in the fridge for up to 2 weeks.

SUGAR SYRUP

Brush sugar syrup onto sponge to enhance its flavour and moistness. Use according to its taste or texture, however don't use too much or the sponge will become overly sweet and sticky.

MATERIALS

❖ 85g (3oz) caster (superfine) sugar

❖ 80ml (2fl oz) water

❖ 1 tsp (5ml) vanilla extract (optional)

EQUIPMENT

❖ Saucepan

❖ Metal spoon

Makes enough for a 20cm (8in) layered round cake (a square cake will need slightly more), 25 fondant fancies or 20–24 cupcakes.

1 Bring the sugar and water to the boil, stirring once or twice. Add the vanilla extract, if using, and leave to cool.

2 Store in an airtight container in the fridge for up to 1 month.

Lemon or orange flavour Replace the water with freshly squeezed, finely strained lemon or orange juice. You can also add a little lemon- or orange-flavoured liqueur (to taste) to heighten the citrus taste.

GANACHE

Made from equal quantities of chocolate and cream, this luxurious filling is silky smooth and rich. Always buy good-quality chocolate with a cocoa solids content of at least 53 per cent. Ganache sets firmer than buttercream at room temperature, so it gives the cake a nice firm surface to ice on, resulting in sharper, cleaner edges and angles. For this reason, I recommend using ganache for all carved/shaped cakes, such as the *Classic Sewing Machine* and *Rotary Dial Telephone*.

Makes about 500g (1lb 2oz); enough for an 18–20cm (7–8in) round or square layer cake, or 20–24 cupcakes.

MATERIALS	EQUIPMENT
❖ 250g (9oz) plain (semisweet or bittersweet) chocolate, chopped, or callets	❖ Saucepan
	❖ Mixing bowl
	❖ Spatula
❖ 250g (9oz) double (heavy) cream	

1 Put the chocolate in a bowl.

2 Bring the cream to the boil in a saucepan, then pour over the chocolate. Stir until the chocolate has all melted and is perfectly combined with the cream.

3 Leave to cool and then cover and store in the fridge. It will keep refrigerated for up to 1 week.

White chocolate ganache

Another sumptuous filling, this makes an ideal alternative to buttercream for using to fill heavy sponge cakes – that is, those that have been made with extra flour. Simply follow the *Ganache* recipe but use the same quantity of white chocolate in place of the plain (semisweet or bittersweet) chocolate and half the amount of cream. If you are making a small batch, melt the white chocolate before mixing it with the hot cream.

TIP

Ensure that your ganache or buttercream is at room temperature before using it – you may even need to warm it slightly before spreading it.

BAKING AND COVERING TECHNIQUES

LAYERING, FILLING AND PREPARATION

To achieve smooth and neatly shaped professional-looking cakes, preparing the cake in the right way ready for icing is essential. Sponge cakes usually consist of two or three layers (see *Classic Sponge Cake*), while fruit cakes are kept whole (see *Traditional Fruit Cake*).

MATERIALS

❖ Buttercream or ganache (see *Fillings and Coverings*) for filling and covering

❖ Sugar syrup (see *Fillings and Coverings*) for brushing

❖ Jam or conserve (preserves) for filling (optional)

EQUIPMENT

❖ Cake leveller

❖ Large serrated knife

❖ Ruler

❖ Small sharp paring knife (optional)

❖ Cake board, plus chopping board or large cake board if needed

❖ Turntable

❖ Palette knives

❖ Pastry brush

1 Cut the dark-baked crust from the base of your cakes. If you have two sponges of equal depths, use a cake leveller to cut them to the same height. If you have baked one-third of your cake mixture in one tin and two-thirds in the other, cut two layers from the deeper sponge with a large serrated knife or cake leveller to make three layers. Alternatively, cut three layers from a larger square cake: cut a round from two opposite quarters of the square close to the corners for two layers, then a semicircle from the other two opposite quarters and piece together for the third layer. Your finished cake will be on a 1.25cm (½in) cake board, so the height of your layers together should be about 9cm (3½in) deep.

2 You should have either baked your cake 2.5cm (1in) larger all round than required or baked a larger sponge (see *Classic Sponge Cake*). Cut around your cake board (this will be the size of your cake), cutting straight down without angling the knife inwards or outwards. For round cakes, use a small sharp paring knife to do this and for square cakes use a large serrated one.

3 Place your three layers of sponge together to check that they are all even and level, trimming away any sponge if necessary. Place your base cake board on a turntable. If the board is smaller than the turntable, put a chopping board or another large cake board underneath. Use a non-slip mat if necessary.

4 Using a medium-size palette knife, spread a small amount of buttercream or ganache onto the cake board and stick down your bottom layer of sponge. Brush sugar syrup over the cake – the quantity depends on how moist you want your cake to be.

5 Spread an even layer of buttercream or ganache about 3mm (⅛in) thick over the sponge, then a thin layer of jam or conserve, if using any. Repeat this procedure for the next layer. Finish by adding the top layer and brushing with more sugar syrup.

6 Cover the side of the cake in buttercream or ganache, then the top – you only need a very thin and even layer. If the coating becomes 'grainy' as it picks up cake crumbs, place in the fridge for about 15 minutes to set and then add a thin second coat. This undercoat is referred to as a 'crumb coat' and helps to seal the sponge.

7 Refrigerate your prepared cake for 20 minutes–1 hour to firm it up, before attempting to cover it with icing or marzipan.

TIP

Try not to add too much filling between the layers of sponge, as the cake will sink slightly under the weight of the icing and ridges will appear.

Filling and covering quantities

Size	10cm (4in)	13cm (5in)	15cm (6in) 8–9 cupcakes	18cm (7in)	20cm (8in)	23cm (9in)	25cm (10in)	28cm (11in)
Buttercream or ganache	175g (6oz)	250g (9oz)	350g (12oz)	500g (1lb 2oz)	650g (1lb 7oz)	800g (1lb 12oz)	1.1kg (2lb 7oz)	1.25kg (2lb 12oz)

CARVING AND SCULPTING CAKES

A few of the cakes in this book involve carving and sculpting the sponge to create a shape other than your classic round or square. I prefer to use ganache rather than buttercream, both for the filling and to coat the outside of the cake, to achieve a much firmer foundation on which to lay the icing.

It is much easier to carve and sculpt cakes when they are very firm or almost frozen, so wrap in clingfilm (plastic wrap) and chill in the freezer beforehand. This technique is used for *Dressed to Impress*, *Rotary Dial Telephone* and the *Classic Sewing Machine*, and also to some extent the *Mantle Clock Masterpiece* and *Classic Jewellery Box*, although these are a little less tricky to tackle. Specific instructions are given for each of these within the project instructions.

When you carve or sculpt your cake, cut the sponge away little by little to prevent yourself from removing too much, especially if you are a beginner. Once you have achieved the desired shape, cover the cake with ganache or buttercream if you prefer, filling in any holes as you go. If the cake becomes crumbly or you are finding it hard to achieve a shape that you are happy with, place it in the fridge for 15 minutes or so, then give it a second coating. This should improve the finish and make the shape more defined. Refrigerate until set and firm enough to cover with icing.

COVERING WITH MARZIPAN AND SUGARPASTE

Before icing, your cake should be covered with a smooth layer of buttercream or ganache (see *Layering, Filling and Preparation*) to ensure that any irregularities or imperfections have been concealed or corrected, otherwise they will be visible through the icing. You can cover cakes with a second coat of icing if necessary, or cover with a layer of marzipan before you ice it with sugarpaste (rolled fondant).

Round cakes

MATERIALS
* Marzipan (optional)
* Sugarpaste (rolled fondant)
* Icing (confectioners') sugar, for dusting (optional)

EQUIPMENT
* Greaseproof (wax) paper or baking (parchment) paper
* Scissors
* Large non-stick rolling pin
* Large non-stick board with non-slip mat (optional)
* Icing and marzipan spacers
* Needle scriber
* Icing smoother
* Small sharp knife

1 Cut a piece of greaseproof or baking paper about 7.5cm (3in) larger all round than your cake and put the cake on top.

2 Knead your marzipan or sugarpaste until soft. Roll it out with a large non-stick rolling pin on a large non-stick board, which usually won't need dusting with icing sugar, set over a non-stick mat. Otherwise, just use a work surface dusted with icing sugar. Use the spacers to give you the correct width – about 5mm (³⁄₁₆in). Lift the sugarpaste up with the rolling pin to release it from the board and turn it a quarter turn before laying it back down to roll again. Try to keep it a round shape so that it will fit over your cake easily. Push out any air bubbles that may occur or use a needle scriber to burst them carefully.

3 Pick the sugarpaste up on your rolling pin and lay it over your cake. Quickly but carefully use your hands to smooth it around and down the side of the cake. Pull the sugarpaste away from the side of the cake as you go until you reach the base.

4 When the icing is on, use a smoother in a circular motion to go over the top of the cake. For the side of the cake, work around the cake in forward circular movements, almost cutting the excess paste at the base. Trim the excess with a small sharp knife. Use the smoother to go around the cake one final time to make sure that it's perfectly smooth.

TIP

Sugarpaste soon dries out and cracks, so you need to work quite quickly. Keep any leftover icing well wrapped in a plastic bag to prevent it from drying out.

Square cakes

Icing a square cake is done in much the same way as a round cake, but take extra care with the corners to prevent the icing from tearing. Gently cup the icing in your hands around the corners before you start working it down the sides of the cake. Any tears in the icing can be mended with clean soft icing, but do this as soon as possible so that it blends in well.

Cake covering quantities

Cake size (9cm/3½in deep)	15cm (6in)	18cm (7in)	20cm (8in)	23cm (9in)	25cm (10in)	28cm (11in)
Marzipan/ sugarpaste (rolled fondant)	650g (1lb 7oz)	750g (1lb 10oz)	850g (1lb 14oz)	1kg (2lb 4oz)	1.25kg (2lb 12oz)	1.5kg (3lb 5oz)

Note: Allow slightly more for square cakes.

SECURING RIBBON AROUND CAKES AND BOARDS

To secure ribbon around the base of a cake, first measure how long the ribbon needs to be by wrapping it around the cake so that it overlaps by about 1cm (⅜in). Trim to length with a sharp pair of scissors. Attach double-sided tape to either end of the ribbon on the same side. Stick one end directly in place onto the icing, then wrap the ribbon around the cake and stick the other end, overlapping, onto the first end.

For professional results, attach double-faced satin ribbon around the edge of the cake board in a matching or complementary colour. Use 1.5cm (⅝in) wide ribbon and secure at intervals around the board with double-sided tape. For square boards, put the double-sided tape around each corner as well as a small piece in the centre of each side.

ICING CAKE BOARDS

Covering the base cake board with icing gives a clean, professional finish to your cake. By carefully choosing the right colour for the icing, the board can be incorporated into the design of the cake itself.

1 Moisten the board with some water. Roll out the sugarpaste (rolled fondant) to 4mm (³⁄₁₆in), ideally using icing or marzipan spacers. Place the board either on a turntable or bring it towards the edge of the work surface. Pick the icing up on the rolling pin and lay it over the cake board so that it is hanging down over it.

2 Use your icing smoother in a downward motion to cut a smooth edge around the board. Cut away any excess icing. Finish by smoothing the top using circular movements to achieve a flat and perfectly smooth surface for your cake to sit on. Leave to dry overnight.

Cake board covering quantities

Cake board size	23cm (9in)	25cm (10in)	28cm (11in)	30cm (12in)	33cm (13in)	35.5cm (14in)
Sugarpaste (rolled fondant)	600g (1lb 5oz)	650g (1lb 7oz)	725g (1lb 9½oz)	850g (1lb 14oz)	1kg (2lb 4oz)	1.2kg (2lb 10½oz)

ASSEMBLING TIERED CAKES

Stacking cakes to create a series of tiers is not a difficult process, but you need to follow the correct procedure to ensure that the cake has a dependable structure. I advise using hollow plastic dowels because of their sturdiness. Thinner plastic dowels are suitable for smaller cakes. See the chart below as a guide to the number of dowels you will need.

MATERIALS
- ❖ Iced cake board (see *Icing Cake Boards*)
- ❖ Stiff royal icing (see *Royal Icing*)

EQUIPMENT
- ❖ Cake-top marking template
- ❖ Needle scriber or marking tool
- ❖ Hollow plastic dowels
- ❖ Edible pen
- ❖ Large serrated knife
- ❖ Spare cake board
- ❖ Spirit level
- ❖ Icing smoothers

1 Use the cake-top marking template to find the centre of your base cake.

2 Using a needle scriber or marking tool, mark the cake where the dowels should go. These need to be positioned well inside the diameter of the cake to be stacked on top. Push a dowel into the cake where it has been marked. Using an edible pen, mark the dowel where it meets the top of the cake.

3 Remove the dowel and cut it at the mark with a large serrated knife. Cut the other dowels to the same height and insert into the cake. Place a cake board on top of the dowels and check that they are equal in height by using a spirit level on the board.

4 Stick your base cake onto the centre of the iced cake board with stiff royal icing. Use your smoothers to move it into position if necessary. Leave the icing to set for a few minutes before stacking on the next tier. Repeat to attach a third tier if needed.

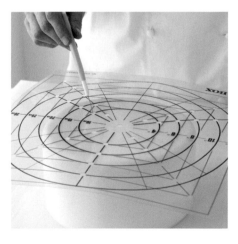  

Dowel quantities

Cake size	15cm (6in)	20cm (8in)	25cm (10in)
No. of dowels	3–4	3–4	4–5

MINI CAKES

Mini cakes are cakes cut from larger pieces of cake that are layered and filled. First, bake a large square cake and from this you can cut out small round or square cakes. The number and size you want will determine the size of the large cake, but it is best to opt for one slightly larger than your requirements to allow for wastage. I make my square mini cakes 5cm (2in), so to make nine you will need an 18cm (7in) square cake. Refer to the charts in the *Cake Recipes* section, but use only two-thirds of the ingredient quantities, as mini cakes are shallower. Bake all the mixture in one tin (pan) rather than dividing it between two for larger cakes.

MATERIALS

✤ Large square baked classic sponge cake or classic chocolate cake (see *Cake Recipes*)

✤ Sugar syrup (see *Fillings and Coverings*)

✤ Buttercream or ganache (see *Fillings and Coverings*)

✤ Sugarpaste (rolled fondant)

EQUIPMENT

✤ Cake leveller

✤ Circle cutter or serrated knife

✤ Pastry brush

✤ Cake card (optional)

✤ Palette knife

✤ Large non-stick rolling pin

✤ Large non-stick board with non-slip mat

✤ Metal ruler

✤ Large sharp knife

✤ Large circle cutter or small sharp knife

✤ Two icing smoothers

Miniature round cakes

1 Slice your large square cake horizontally into two even layers using a cake leveller. Cut small individual rounds with a cutter.

2 Brush the pieces of sponge with sugar syrup and sandwich together with either buttercream (plus jam if desired) or ganache if using a chocolate-flavoured cake. It's easier if you stick the bottom piece of cake to a cake card the same size and shape as your mini cake, using buttercream or ganache, but not essential. Working quickly, pick up each cake and cover the sides evenly with buttercream or ganache. Finish by covering the top and then place the cakes in the fridge for at least 20 minutes to firm up.

TIP

You will find it easier to work with the sponge if it's very cold, as it will be much firmer.

3 Roll out a piece of sugarpaste 38cm (15in) square and 5mm (³⁄₁₆in) thick with a large non-stick rolling pin on a large non-stick board set over a non-slip mat. Cut nine small squares and lay one over each cake. If you are a beginner, prepare half the cakes at a time, keeping the other squares under cling film (plastic wrap) to prevent them from drying out.

4 Use your hands to work the icing down around the sides of the cake and trim away the excess with a large circle cutter.

5 Use two icing smoothers on either side of the cake going forwards and backwards and turning the cake as you go to create a perfectly smooth result. Leave the icing to dry, ideally overnight, before decorating the cakes.

TIP

For mini traditional fruit cakes, bake the mixture in small, individual tins. They can't be cut out due to the structure of the cakes.

Miniature square cakes

Square mini cakes are created in a similar way to the round ones, so follow the instructions above (see *Miniature Round Cakes*). Cut out squares of cake using a serrated knife and use a sharp knife to cut away the excess icing around the sides of the cake. Finish the cakes by using smoothers on opposite sides to press and smooth the icing around the four sides.

BAKING CUPCAKES

The cake mixtures used for baking cupcakes in this book are the same as those used for full-size cakes. Choose from *Classic Sponge Cake*, *Classic Chocolate Cake* or *Carrot Cake* (see *Cake Recipes*). To make a batch of 10–12 cupcakes, use the quantities given for a 13cm (5in) round or 10cm (4in) square cake.

To bake the mixture, place cupcake cases (liners) in tartlet tins (pans) or muffin trays (pans) and fill them two-thirds to three-quarters full. Bake in a preheated oven at 180°C/350°F/Gas Mark 4 for about 20 minutes, until the cakes are springy to the touch.

I prefer to use plain foil cupcake cases (liners), available in a range of colours, because the foil keeps the cakes fresh and there is no pattern to draw attention away from the decoration on the cakes. But they also come in plain or patterned paper, and you can use decorative cases for plainer cupcakes.

COVERING CUPCAKES WITH SUGARPASTE

Sugarpaste (rolled fondant) -covered cupcakes are quick to make. Just use a cutter to cut out a circle of sugarpaste (rolled fondant) and place inside the cupcake top. Use cupcakes that have a nice even, slightly domed shape to them and trim them if necessary.

1 Using a palette knife, spread a thin layer of flavoured buttercream (frosting) or ganache over the cakes so that it forms a perfectly rounded and smooth surface for the icing to sit on.

2 Roll out some sugarpaste (rolled fondant) and, using a circle cutter, cut out circles very slightly bigger than the cupcake top. I would suggest cutting out nine at a time and covering any circles that you are not using with clingfilm (plastic wrap). Cover the cupcakes one at a time, using the palm of your hand to carefully tease the icing out to the edges to completely cover the tops.

BUTTERCREAM-TOPPED CUPCAKES

Topping with buttercream is the quickest and simplest way to ice a cupcake. The cupcakes themselves don't need to be perfectly shaped, as the buttercream topping will hide any imperfections.

1 Before you prepare or ice the cupcakes, make sure they are completely cool. Brush the tops with extra sugar syrup if you think they might be a bit dry or if you want them to be really moist (see *Fillings and Coverings*).

2 You can also 'inject' jams or conserves (preserves) into your sponge before you top them with buttercream. Simply fill a squeezy bottle with a narrow-pointed nozzle with the jam or conserve, carefully insert it into the cupcakes and squeeze.

3 To pipe your cupcakes, fit a large disposable plastic piping (pastry) bag with a large plain or star-shaped tube (tip), fill with buttercream (see *Fillings and Coverings*) and pipe a kiss (peak) or swirl onto the top – it will take a little practice to get each cake looking perfect.

4 Alternatively, simply use a palette knife to spread the buttercream on evenly to create a neat domed top. Make sure your icing is soft when you use it – you may need to re-beat it or even warm it slightly if the room temperature is fairly cold.

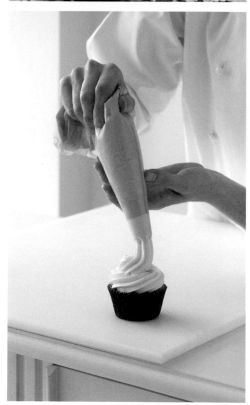

BAKING COOKIES

Suitable for almost every occasion, cookies also give you plenty of creative scope, as you can cut all manner of shapes from the dough and decorate them in many different ways. They also offer an ideal opportunity to involve children in their preparation. Cookies can be made well in advance of the event for added convenience.

MATERIALS
- ❖ 250g (9oz) unsalted butter
- ❖ 250g (9oz) caster (superfine) sugar
- ❖ 1–2 medium eggs
- ❖ 1 tsp (5ml) vanilla extract
- ❖ 500g (1lb 2oz) plain (all-purpose) flour, plus extra for dusting

EQUIPMENT
- ❖ Large electric mixer
- ❖ Spatula
- ❖ Deep tray or plastic container
- ❖ Rolling pin
- ❖ Cookie cutters or templates
- ❖ Sharp knife (if using templates)
- ❖ Baking trays (sheets) lined with greaseproof (wax) paper or baking (parchment) paper

Shelf life
The cookie dough can be made a few days ahead or stored in the freezer until ready to use. The baked cookies will keep for up to one month.

Flavour variations

Chocolate Substitute 50g (1oz) flour with (unsweetened) cocoa.
Citrus Omit the vanilla and add the finely grated zest of 1 lemon or orange.
Almond Replace the vanilla with 1 tsp (5ml) almond extract.

1 In a large electric mixer, beat the butter and sugar together until creamy and quite fluffy.

2 Add the eggs and vanilla extract and mix until they are well combined.

3 Sift the flour, add to the bowl of the mixer and mix until all the ingredients just come together. You may need to do this in two stages – do not over-mix.

4 Tip the dough into a container lined with clingfilm (plastic wrap) and press down firmly. Cover with clingfilm (plastic wrap) and refrigerate for at least 30 minutes.

TIP

Don't add too much flour when you are rolling out your cookies or they will become too dry.

5 On a work surface lightly dusted with flour, roll out the cookie dough to about 4mm (⅜in) thick. Sprinkle a little extra flour on top of the dough as you roll to prevent it from sticking to the rolling pin.

6 Cut out your shapes either with cutters or using templates and a sharp knife. Place on baking trays lined with greaseproof (wax) or baking paper and return to the fridge to rest for at least 30 minutes. Meanwhile, preheat your oven to 180°C/350°F/Gas Mark 4.

7 Bake the cookies for about 10 minutes, depending on their size, or until they are golden brown. Leave them to cool completely before storing them in an airtight container until you are ready to decorate them.

Cookie pops

Cookie pops are so fun to create. Simply bake your cookies following the instructions above, inserting the sticks into the dough before you cut out the shapes. You can't cut through where the stick goes into the dough, so use a knife to carefully cut around that area.

DECORATING TECHNIQUES

ROYAL ICING

Learning to work with royal icing is a one of the most important skills to acquire in cake decorating. Royal icing is such a versatile medium as it can be used for icing cakes and cookies, intricate piping of decorations or simply for attaching and sticking.

Use royal icing while it's as fresh as possible for best results, however it will keep for up to five days when stored an airtight container. If it not used immediately, re-beat the mixture back to its correct consistency before use.

MATERIALS
- ❖ 2 medium egg whites or 15g (½oz) dried egg albumen powder mixed with 75ml (2fl oz) water
- ❖ 500g (1lb 2oz) icing (confectioners') sugar

EQUIPMENT
- ❖ Large electric mixer
- ❖ Sieve (strainer)
- ❖ Spatula

1 If using dried egg powder, soak it in the water for at least 30 minutes in advance, but ideally overnight in the fridge.

2 Sift the icing sugar into the bowl of a large electric mixer and add the egg whites or strained reconstituted egg mixture.

3 Mix together on a low speed for about 3–4 minutes until the icing has reached a stiff-peak consistency, which is what you need for sticking on decorations and gluing cakes together.

4 Store the icing in an airtight container covered with a damp, clean cloth to prevent it from drying out.

Soft-peak royal icing

To pipe decorations easily, you may need to add a tiny amount of water to your royal icing to soften it slightly.

RUN-OUT ICING

Royal icing is thinned down with water to 'flood' cookies (see *Royal-Iced Cookies*). Test for the desired consistency by lifting your spoon and letting the icing drip back into the bowl – it should remain on the surface for five seconds before disappearing. If it's too runny it will run over the outlines and sides of the cookies, but if it's too stiff it won't spread very well.

MAKING A PIPING BAG

1 Cut two equal triangles from a large square of greaseproof (wax) paper or baking (parchment) paper. As a guide, for small piping (pastry) bags cut from a 15–20cm (6–8in) square and for large bags cut from a 30–35.5cm (12–14in) square.

2 If right-handed, keeping the centre point towards you with the longest side farthest away, curl the right-hand corner inwards and bring the point to meet the centre point. Adjust your hold so the two points are together between right thumb and index finger.

3 With your left hand, curl the left point inwards, bringing it across the front and around to the back of the other two points in the centre of the cone. Adjust your grip so that you are holding the three points together with both thumbs and index fingers. Tighten the cone by gently rubbing your thumb and index fingers forwards and backwards until you have a sharp tip at the end of the bag.

4 Carefully fold the back of the bag (where all the points meet) inwards and press hard along the fold. Repeat to secure.

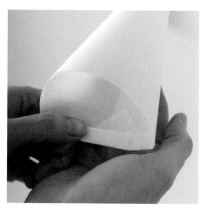

TIP

Make lots of piping bags at a time and put them aside for a decorating session.

PIPING WITH ROYAL ICING

For basic piping work, use soft-peak royal icing (see *Royal Icing*). The size of the tube (tip) you use will depend on the job at hand.

Fill the piping (pastry) bag until it is no more than one-third full. Fold the top over, away from the join, until you have a tight and well-sealed bag. The correct way to hold the piping (pastry) bag is important. Use your index finger to guide the bag. You can also use your other hand to guide you if it's easier.

To pipe dots, squeeze the icing out gently until you have the dot that's the size you want. Stop squeezing then lift the bag. If there is a peak in the icing, use a damp brush to flatten it down.

To pipe teardrops, once you have squeezed out the dot, pull the tube (tip) through the dot, then release the pressure and lift the bag. To pipe elongated teardrops and swirls, squeeze out a ball of icing and drag the icing round to one side to form a swirl or scroll. Increase the pressure and amount of icing you squeeze out for longer, larger shapes. Keeping close to the surface you are piping on is known as 'scratch piping'.

To pipes lines, touch the tube (tip) down, then lift the bag up in a smooth movement, squeezing gently. Decrease the pressure and touch it back down to the point where you want the line to finish. Try not to drag the icing along, or it will become uneven. Use a template or a cookie outline as a guide where possible.

To pipe a 'snail trail' border, squeeze out a large dot of icing and drag the tube (tip) through it to one side like a teardrop. Repeat this motion around the cake.

To 'drop in' icing, 'drop' a different coloured, runny icing into the flooding icing (see *Run-out Icing*) while it is still wet. This gives a slightly different and more blended effect, rather than just piping directly onto the top of the dry cookie.

ROYAL-ICED COOKIES

This is my favourite method of icing cookies, as I love the taste of the crisp white icing against the softer texture of the cookie underneath. If you are icing a large quantity of cookies, use a squeezable plastic bottle with a small tube (tip) instead of piping bags.

MATERIALS
❖ Soft-peak royal icing (see *Royal Icing*)

EQUIPMENT
❖ Small and large paper piping bags (see *Making a Piping Bag*)
❖ Piping tubes (tips) nos. 1.5 or 2 and 1

1 Place the no. 1.5 or 2 tube in a small paper piping bag and fill with some soft-peak royal icing. Pipe an outline around the edge of each cookie, or the area that you wish to ice.

2 Thin down some more royal icing with water until 'flooding' consistency (see *Run-Out Icing*) and place in a large paper piping bag fitted with a no. 1 tube. Use to flood inside the outlines on the cookies with icing. For larger cookies, you can snip off the end of the bag instead of using a tube. If the area you need to flood is relatively large, work around the edges of the piped outline and then inwards to the centre to ensure an even covering.

3 Once dry, pipe over any details that are required and stick on decorations as desired.

COVERING COOKIES WITH SUGARPASTE

For neat and professional cookies that are very quick to ice, simply roll out some sugarpaste (rolled fondant) to no more than 3mm (⅛in) thick and cut out the shape of the cookie with the same cutter or template used for cutting out the cookies from the cookie dough. Stick the cut-out icing shapes onto the cookies using boiled and cooled apricot masking spread or strained jam, taking care not to stretch and distort the icing.

WORKING WITH FLOWER PASTE

Flower (petal/gum) paste is used successfully for creating delicate icing decorations for cakes and cookies, such as flowers, frills and bows, as it can be rolled out very thinly. Before using the paste, knead it thoroughly by continuously pulling it apart with your fingers.

MODELLING PASTE AND CMC

Modelling paste is similar to sugarpaste (rolled fondant), only stiffer in consistency, which allows you to mould larger, more robust shapes and decorations. It isn't as strong and doesn't dry out as quickly as flower (petal/gum) paste. You can buy modelling paste ready-made, but it's cost-effective and very easy to make your own using CMC (sodium carboxymethyl cellulose), which comes in the form of a powder that you knead into sugarpaste. As a guide, use about 1 teaspoon (5ml) per 300g (10oz) icing.

COLOURING ICINGS

There are different kinds of food colouring available: paste, liquid, gel and dust. I prefer to use paste for colouring sugarpaste (rolled fondant), flower (petal/gum) paste and marzipan because it prevents the icing from becoming wet and sticky. Add small amounts with a cocktail stick (toothpick) and larger amounts with a knife and then knead it into the icing. Always add colouring gradually, keeping some extra white icing to hand in case you add too much colour. Liquid food colour is good for colouring royal icing and liquid fondant, but be careful not to add too much too soon. Be aware that the colour of icing can change as it dries – some colours tend to fade while others darken.

TIP

It's best to colour more icing than you need to allow for mishaps. Any leftovers can be stored in an airtight bag in a sealed container.

USING SUGARVEIL

Sugarveil is another type of icing, mainly used to create extremely delicate, paper-thin pieces of sugar lace to decorate cakes, cookies and other confectionery. These pieces are made by smearing wet icing into moulded, silicone mats, leaving it to dry for up to a few hours and carefully teasing it out to reveal a finely detailed patterned sheet. Sugarveil has been a great addition to projects in this book, such as the *Beautiful Bridal Lace* cake and *Classic Sewing Machine*, as the exquisite traditional lace patterns instantly enhance the vintage theme.

The instructions are written clearly on the packet, but here they are again just in case! Always prepare the Sugarveil 24 hours before you need it.

MATERIALS
❖ Sugarveil powder
❖ 120ml (3¼fl oz) boiling water

EQUIPMENT
❖ Electric mixer fitted with whisk attachment
❖ Sugarveil scraper
❖ Mat (I use Rose Mantilla for all projects in this book)

1 Place the contents of the packet into a bowl of an electric mixer. Add the boiling water and mix it briefly into the powder with a spoon. Then mix with the whisk attachment at high speed for four minutes.

2 After four minutes the icing should be slightly stiff and quite white, almost like a meringue mix. Spoon the mix into a bowl and wrap with cling film or keep in a small container with a lid in the fridge overnight.

3 Smear a couple of spoonfuls of Sugarveil onto your mat and use the Sugarveil scraper to spread the icing in different directions to ensure that it gets into all of the crevasses. Remove any excess Sugarveil and clean the side of the mat and the scraper with a clean damp cloth.

4 Use the Sugarveil scraper to complete one last scrape across the mat, from one end to the other. Set the mat aside to dry for about 3–6 hours – the drying time will depend on how humid it is.

5 Once the icing is no longer tacky and the corners can be easily teased away, it is ready to be peeled away from the mat.

6 To peel the icing out, tease out one side and turn the mat face down. Use the Sugarveil scraper the hold the icing down on the bench then peel back the mould (peeling the mould from the Sugarveil, rather than the Sugarveil from the mould).

7 Store the Sugarveil between sheets of greaseproof (wax) paper in an airtight container for up to 2–3 days. The wet mix can be stored in the fridge for up to one week.

USING MOULDS

Moulds are really useful for creating intricately detailed and lifelike details, such as jewels, pearls and brooches. There are so many now on the market and although they are quite expensive, they are very durable if looked after properly. They are really versatile too and it's fun experimenting with the effects you can achieve. Often you get a few different shapes on one mould and you can even use a certain part of the mould, rather than the whole thing.

Silicone moulds work best as you can peel the icing out more easily without spoiling the shape. To prevent the icing from sticking, you will need to either grease the mould slightly with Trex (white vegetable fat) before use or brush dust or lustre into it.

Templates

Download full-size, printable templates at
http://ideas.stitchcraftcreate.co.uk/patterns

Designer Art Deco

Symmetrical Shapes Cake A, B, C, D, E and F

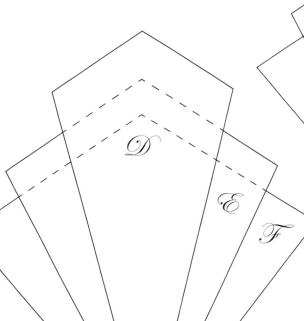

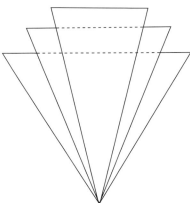

Geometric Mini Cakes G, H, I

Sew Stylish

Classic Sewing Machine A, B, C

A and B shown at 50%, enlarge by 200%

Shown at 50%, enlarge by 200%

Fifties Dress

Dressed to Impress Dress shape

*Shown at 50%,
enlarge by 200%*

Little Black Dress Front, back and sleeves

Front and
back

Sleeve

*Both shown at 50%,
enlarge by 200%*

Antique Timepieces

Mantel Clock Masterpiece Victorian
Bauble (ornament)

Mantel Clock Masterpiece
Clock base

Dusky Lace Dream

Beautiful Bridal Lace and **Floral Lace Cookies**

Large flower
Shown at 50%, enlarge by 200%

Traditional Telephones

Retro Phone Cookies Phone shape

*Shown at 50%,
enlarge by 200%*

Both shown at 50%, enlarge by 200%

The Charleston

Fabulous Feathers Cake Feathers

Fun Feather Mini cakes Feathers

Both shown at 50%, enlarge by 200%

Beautiful Hatboxes

Simple Rose Hatbox Large and small roses

Vintage Hat Cookies
Hats

Romantic Rose Hatbox
Large rose, Small rose

Suppliers

UK

THE CAKE PARLOUR
www.thecakeparlour.com
146 Arthur Road, Wimbledon Park,
London SW19 8AQ
Tel: 020 8947 4424

A PIECE OF CAKE
www.sugaricing.com
18–20 Upper High Street, Thame,
Oxon OX9 3EX
Tel: 01844 213428

CAKES 4 FUN
www.cakes4fun.co.uk
100 Lower Richmond Road, Putney,
London SW15 1LN
Tel: 020 8785 9039

SQUIRE'S KITCHEN SHOP
www.squires-shop.com
3 Waverley Lane, Farnham,
Surrey GU9 8BB
Tel: 0845 6171810

SUGARSHACK
www.sugarshack.co.uk
Unit 12, Bowman Trading Estate,
Westmoreland Road,
London NW9 9RL
Tel: 020 8204 2994

**THE CAKE DECORATING
COMPANY
(FOR STENCILS AND SUGARVEIL)**
www.thecakedecoratingcompany.
co.uk
Shop 2B, Triumph Road,
Nottingham
Tel: 0115 822 4521

US

DESIGNER STENCILS
www.designerstencils.com
2503 Silverside Road,
Wilmington DE 19810
Tel: 800-822-7836

GLOBAL SUGAR ART
www.globalsugarart.com
1509 Military Turnpike, Plattsburgh,
New York 12901
Tel: 1-518-561-3039

Australia

BAKERY SUGARCRAFT
www.bscretail.com.au
198 Newton Road, Wetherill Park,
Sydney 2164
Tel: 02 9828 0700

GLASSHOUSE CAKE SUPPLIES
www.glasshousecakes.com.au
13B Selems Parade,
Revesby NSW 2212
Tel: 02 9773 5513

Acknowledgments

Thanks again to my fabulous and talented team behind the design and production of this book:
to Sarah Underhill for her creative eye and styling and to Mark Scott for the amazing photography.
Thanks to Beth Dymond for all the help and patience with the editing and to David & Charles for
the support and encouragement they have given me to complete this book.

I would like to thank Nonsuch Mansions (**www.nonsuchmansion.com**) and White Location
(**www.whitelocation.co.uk**) for allowing us to shoot in their beautiful venues, The Crockery
Cupboard for letting me using their beautiful plates and Zita Elze for the flowers.

I'd also like to thank Kaysie Lackey for her wonderful class recently that gave me so much
inspiration to create designs using new techniques, which for me was very important for this book.

Finally, I'd like to thank my wonderful friends, staff, students and my family for all their love, help
and support always.

About the Author

Zoe Clark is one of London's leading cake designers, and her work regularly appears in the UK's bestselling bridal and sugarcraft magazines. Her cake designs have also featured on television and in films, and she has previously produced four books for D&C showcasing her unique style. Zoe opened The Cake Parlour in South West London in November 2010, where as well as offering a bespoke cake and confectionery design service for every occasion she also runs cake-decorating classes for aspiring cake decorators from all over the country and beyond. Zoe has recently started supplying the world-renowned Fortnum & Mason store with an exclusive range of wedding and celebration cakes and cookies.

www.thecakeparlour.com
www.zoeclarkcakes.com

Index

A DAVID & CHARLES BOOK
© F&W Media International, Ltd 2013

David & Charles is an imprint of F&W Media
International, Ltd
Brunel House, Forde Close, Newton Abbot,
TQ12 4PU, UK

F&W Media International, Ltd is a subsidiary of
F+W Media, Inc
10151 Carver Road, Cincinnati OH45242, USA

Text and Designs © Zoe Clark 2013
Layout and Photography © F&W Media International,
Ltd 2013

First published in the UK and USA in 2013

Names of manufacturers and product ranges are
provided for the information of readers, with no
intention to infringe copyright or trademarks.

A catalogue record for this book is available from the
British Library.

ISBN-13: 978-1-4463-0284-2 hardback
ISBN-10: 1-4463-0284-9 hardback

ISBN-13: 978-1-4463-0285-9 paperback
ISBN-10: 1-4463-0285-7 paperback

Printed in China by RR Donnelley for:
F&W Media International, Ltd
Brunel House, Forde Close, Newton Abbot,
TQ12 4PU, UK

10 9 8 7 6 5 4 3 2 1

Publisher: Alison Myer
Craft Business Manager: Ame Verso
Junior Acquisitions Editor: James Brooks
Project Editor: Beth Dymond
Art Editor: Sarah Underhill
Photographer: Mark Scott
Senior Production Controller: Kelly Smith

F+W Media publishes high quality books on a wide
range of subjects.
For more great book ideas visit:
www.stitchcraftcreate.co.uk